40:LANDSCAPES

JAMES GRAYSON TRULOVE

40:LANDSCAPES

JAMES GRAYSON TRULOVE

THUNDER BAY
P·R·E·S·S

San Diego, California

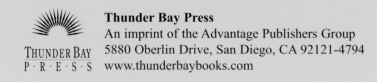

Thunder Bay Press
An imprint of the Advantage Publishers Group
5880 Oberlin Drive, San Diego, CA 92121-4794
www.thunderbaybooks.com

All notations of errors or omissions should be addressed to Thunder Bay Press, Editorial Department, at the above address. All other correspondence (author inquiries, permissions) concerning the content of this book should be addressed to Rockport Publishers, Inc., 33 Commercial Street, Gloucester, MA 01930-5089. Telephone: (978) 283-9590; Fax: (978) 283-2742; www.rockpub.com

ISBN: 1-59223-096-2

Library of Congress Cataloging-in-Publication data available upon request.

1 2 3 4 5 07 06 05 04 03

Cover Image:

Front cover:
Top row: Topher Delaney/Topher Delaney, Inc., Seam Studio (left); Ira Nowinski/Topher Delaney, Inc., Seam Studio

Second row: Ira Nowinski/Topher Delaney, Inc., Seam Studio (left); Kelli Yon/Topher Delaney, Inc., Seam Studio (second left); Ian Reeves/Topher Delaney, Inc., Seam Studio (second right); Minao Tabata/Shunmyo Masuno (right)

Third row: Gabriel Figueroa/Mario Schjetnan (left); Kelli Yon/Topher Delaney, Inc., Seam Studio (second left); Michael & James Balston/Balston & Company (second right); Lanny Provo/Raymond Jungles, Inc. (right)

Fourth row: Minao Tabata/Shunmyo Masuno

Fifth row: Ira Nowinski/Topher Delaney, Inc., Seam Studio (left); Michael & James Balston/Balston & Company (second left); Haruo Hirota/ Shunmyo Masuno (second right); Minao Tabata/Shunmyo Masuno (right)

Back cover: Michael & James Balston/Balston & Company (top left); Haruo Hirota/ Shunmyo Masuno (bottom right)

Printed in China

CONTENTS

Projects

REVERSING THE PLANES OF PERCEPTION

STAMPER GARDEN

ABOVE: *Detail of "Rail of Perception"*
LEFT: *The vessel of water is submerged into a flat plane of grass punctuated by the thick trunk of birch.*
OPPOSITE PAGE ABOVE: *A cantilevered French limestone deck extends twenty feet over the existing grade.*
OPPOSITE PAGE BELOW: *Vertical rail pickets lay down in shadow across the French limestone terrace.*

ABOVE: *Spa with vertical glass wall. The surface of the water acts as a mutable mirror reflecting the picturesque.*
OPPOSITE PAGE: *Black academy granite forms a boundary installation by Edwin Hamilton. The graceful movement and texture of* Miscanthus gracillimus *contrasts the structural forms of stone.*

The focus of the garden's core is the "wild" land beyond the boundary of the internal geometric precision of limestone, grass, and water. This private garden, a mosaic of horizontal physical planes constitutes a viewing platform to the surrounding external public lands. the genesis of the spiritual philosophy which guides the formation of this garden is the obverse of the traditional walled sanctuary garden. The act of contemplation "of viewing" is expanded from the boundary of personal ownership, the edge of the suspended terrace, to a boundless panorama of "the wild." Here on this controlled green plinth of land one can meditate upon the uncontrolled complexity and beauty of the external. The intent of this internal garden is to recognize the extraordinary surrounding landmass through the literal elimination of the horizontal plane. Depending on one's angle of observation, the vertical pickets form a fan of visual perceptions from the open "invisible" to a solid boundary of definitions.

Within the frame of the ground plane a pool of water is set to form a horizontal surface which constantly ripples shifting the reflections of the sky. This body of water mirrors a streaming sequence of imagery which continually activates the core of the garden.

Adjacent to the entry garden, the threshold of transition between "the wild", the public woods, and the "ordered/controlled" private garden of contemplation is formed by the stacking of the wood removed through the original clearing of the land. The wall translates the process of removal/clearing and retrieval/reconstitution—the ultimate process of the garden—removal of the wild (nature untamed) and retrieval of nature tamed, the reformation of land into a syllabus of ornament, a style, the formal intervention of a garden.

OPPOSITE PAGE: *Detail of entrance wall.*
ABOVE: *Entrance sculptural stone wall by Edwin Hamilton.*

Stamper Garden

P A S S A G E

T O T H E P R E S E N C E O F T H A T W H I C H I S A B S E N T

GREENWICH GARDEN

THE MEASURE OF ELEVATIONS

MEASURE OF THE LINE
ACROSS THE GRADIENT
DESCENDING
ASCENDING
DETERMINED BY THE ROOT OF THE NATURAL FULCRUM

This sequence of images depicts a cross section of land in three dimensions descending through the layered contours, a thin metallic strip of stainless steel demarks the "cross", further descent reveals the section—this manufactured geometry reinforces the placement of the vertical trunk of the central form of growth. This is the geometry of topography both in the vertical and the horizontal.

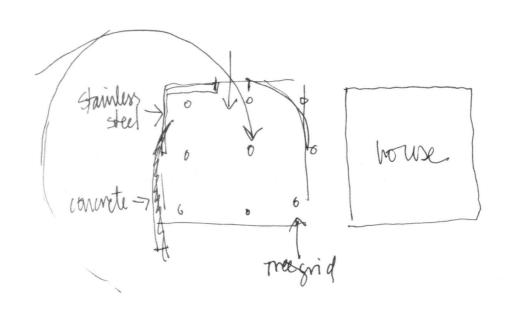

stainless steel →

concrete →

house

treegrid

ABOVE AND RIGHT: *In a physical reference to the geometric art of Russian Constructivism, the central plane of the auto court is defined by the geometry of "the angle" and "the arc". A sixty foot white concrete arcing plane bisects the angle of a tangent of a stainless steel reticular form. Expanding from the core plane are overlapping arcs of stainless steel, boxwood, and radiating tangents of honed and polished granite.*

OPPOSITE PAGE: *The entrance is defined by a vector of asphalt and concrete which lodges into the form of the granite circle.*

Descending on the curve of the driveway, one passes through tangents of a boxwood circle to arrive within a central court defined by geometric forms. A pristine stainless steel triangular panel bisects a sixty-foot white concrete arcing plane. A seam of grass, Calmagrostis "Karl Forster" rises up between the intersection of these manufactured forms, a gesture, an act, which reflects the cycle of the seasons. Nine *Fagus sylvatica atropurpurea* are planted in a grid over-laying these discrete layers of metal and concrete modules to form a complex canopy of dappled branch patterns.

Tangentially located, the main entrance is paved in a compendium of geometric forms: honed granite and stainless steel. Longitudinal forms bisect the circle, a metaphor for the whole family infused with energy, the bisection of the line entering the sacred space.

In the rear garden, enveloped by the surrounding woods is a descending series of grass terraces punctuated by a triangle of stainless steel, arresting the flow of the arcs directly in front of the vertical form of the core/trunk of the largest tree. The gray furrowed bark of this tree, imperceptibly transforming with each season, contrasts with the immutable polished surface of the stainless triangle—a plinth of industry upholding the form of nature. Swaths of sedum, lavender, and chartreuse *Alchemilla mollis* roil the clipped surface and texture of the geometric ground planes of lawn. The device of the wall, the line of demarcation at the high point of the land, coupled with one's movement descending down around the "line", reveals the sculptural shift of the wall. This repetitive gesture in/on the land of the elevational modulations refers to the traditional device of the "HA HA", transformed in a contemporary interpretation of elevation—how we and from where we view a site—the shift of perception.

HATCH GARDEN

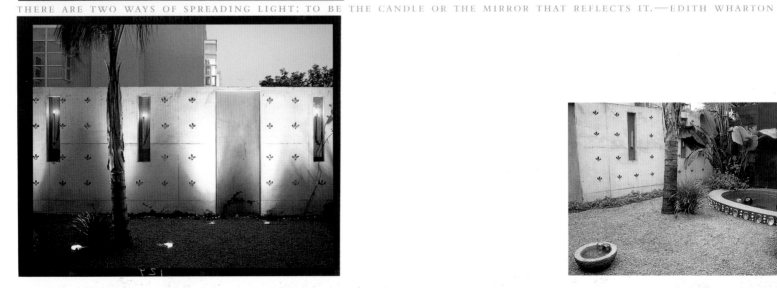

THERE ARE TWO WAYS OF SPREADING LIGHT: TO BE THE CANDLE OR THE MIRROR THAT REFLECTS IT. —EDITH WHARTON

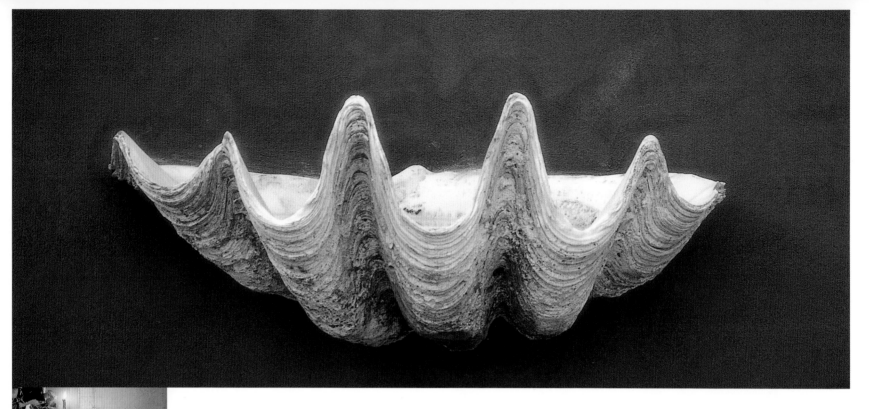

This white concrete wall defines the reality of two gardens considered and consummated at the same exact point in time. On the east side we developed "the garden of revelation" and on the west side we developed the Hatch garden. The physical form of the wall states by its very essence a proclamation of distinct individual interpretations: in contrast to clipped balls of boxwood on the east side, the west side is ornamented with mussel shells and mirrors set in a fleur de lys pattern. The glow of suspended candles emanates from the sienna and sulphur stained recessed niches.

Queen palms flutter their shadows on the text planes of the walls. The spa, the locus of abulations, is encrusted with shells patterned in a maritime jewel motif. Water flows over the extraordinary proportions of sculptural shells embedded in the violet walls. The foliage of giant birds of paradise fan the oval form of the spa. The wood walls, stained green, form the frame for white wisteria as it twists and whirls across the formal lines of the vertical plane. There is a sense of tranquility—the rustle of palm fronds, the sound of the water as it flows from a mysterious spring to an aqueous source of rejuvenation, the smell of citrus and roses, the flicker of candle light illuminating the sienna niches all contribute to form a cloistered sanctuary within the density of urban construction.

ABOVE: *The suspended shell is an allusion to the fonts found at the entrance to spiritual sanctuaries. The act of taking the water and blessing oneself is transferred to the act of literally washing the entire bod within "the spa." The shell is the well spring—the font of "purity"—pure water—thus in both a spiritual and sensual sense our equilibrium is restored through the experience of being in the garden.*
OPPOSITE INSET: *Oil sketch of the garden done as a study for the actual construction drawings.*

GARDEN OF

PACIFIC GARDEN

ABSTRACT GEOMETRY

PREVIOUS PAGE LEFT: *Sculptural trumpets of light hang from the eucalyptus; a diaphanous stainless steel rail etches the edge of the deck of the upper public garden.*

PREVIOUS PAGE RIGHT UPPER: *Grass emanates from the top of the black stucco wall.*

previous page right middle and lower: *The geometric shift of wood and concrete rectangles on axis descend down the curve of the steps.*

BELOW: *Detail of "the discrete shift."*

OPPOSITE PAGE *The sequence of the geometric shift from public to private garden. On the north side of the steps an arced canted blue concrete wall lined with grasses and on the south a curving black stucco wall form the aperture of descent. No rails are required because the ground level has been elevated to step tread.*

This south facing urban garden, separated by a shift in elevation of fifteen feet, serves as a sanctuary for two distinct relationships: one of an immediate direct public nature and one of a sequestered intimate nature. On the upper elevation sweeping past six sets of French doors, a deck of ipe wood extends the flow of movement across the threshold of the internal to the external. Quite literally doors open to a room with a view. Suspended from the thick, gnarled trunk of the overhanging eucalyptus are fiberglass light cones which sway in the breeze creating animated circles of light on the surface of the deck. Planted to create privacy, surrounding this platform of wood, is a massing of *Bambusa oldhamii*, white Sombrieul roses, white Calla lilies, honey-suckle and ginger. A finely detailed stainless steel rail rims the curve of the deck, which is capped by a broad, flat band of stainless steel, on which to rest one's elbows, contemplating the sinuous shift from the macro view to the micro view of the garden.

Two curving sculptural walls of colored stucco frame the descent from the deck platform to the stone terrace adjacent to the pool. To the south of this serpentine staircase is a black wall which is bisected to create "a discrete shift"—an aperture through which to view the splaying arc of a blue concrete bench. A tufted line of grass emanates from the top of this wall with no apparent connection to the earth—a curious visual conundrum. Embedded in the text of descending steps is an intricate geometric text. Ipe wood laid on axis to both the black wall and the curve of the descent is enveloped by a black concrete square which is revealed in the descent. The corner of the concrete axis lifts to a form a triangle seat—pop-up geometry. Scented opulent trumpets of Brugmansia's white flowers hang over the canted blue concrete boundary wall of the descending steps.

OPPOSITE PAGE: *Canted and arcing concrete bench. Red lava dust and oil paving inset with variegated geraniums and sedum.*

Magenta bougainvillaea, lemons, bamboo, bananas, and gardenias envelop the lower garden. Anchoring the four-corners of the pool are concrete vessels planted with palms. The bottom of the pool is filled with loose blue pebbles, which diffuses the internal edges of the surfaces. The choice of palms reflects the visual repetition of an existing palm, which rises majestically up on the adjacent property. In the evening, the lower garden is defined by Chinese hanging lanterns, which emit orbs of soft yellow light creating a sense of an impending romantic celebration. Every night, a story is woven in the garden of Scheherazade.

OPPOSITE PAGE: *The cloistered garden enveloped by a rim of bamboo, bouganvillaea, solanum, and ivy. Necorema and jasmin in foreground flank the swimming pool. Suspended handmade Chinese lanterns cast a glow over the garden.*

GUPTA GARDEN

POINT OF VIEW—A BIAS OF INTERPRETATION IN RELATION TO TIME AND SPACE.

PREVIOUS PAGE LEFT: *Detail of wall with pink geraniums selected to emphasize the coloration of the vertical surfaces.*
PREVIOUS PAGE RIGHT: *Detail of circular wall with desert palm gravel. A niche placed directly at apex of the circle reveals "nature" growing rampant behind the wall.*
ABOVE: *Detail of rastra foam wall finished with integrally colored acrylic stucco.* Salvia leucantha *is planted as a cameo appearance of beauty in form, color, and texture. The aperture in the circle leads to an elevated garden of lavender, black sand, and eclectic perennials.*
OPPOSITE PAGE: *Dark blue stucco wall projects through the wall calling into question the discrete separation of volumetric garden rooms. This form signals the movement from one elevation to another.*

The Release

"When you had finished plastering the colors on the walls, I had a dream—that wild animals were twisting in motion."

"The fire colors are vibrant expressions, especially the orange and red hues. Fire is an important part of my life. It is a dynamic element in the equation of life. Fire is mutable. You can feed it and watch it grow. It is interactive, a dynamic form of interchange."

Paul places front and center a brazier, which burns (in control/under control), creating mutable shafts of light on the orange surfaces of the circular enclosure.

The Frame

This is both a pictorial garden (the frame of the garden) and a sensual garden (the immersion in the garden), which is appreciated from the physical internal home space and the visual internal— the eye of the beholder.

"I am always assessing the modulations of this space, which transports me to the sacred space of a unique sanctuary." —Paul Gupta

LEFT: *The circular garden room is located directly in front of the main living area which frames the central court garden in a wrap of vibrant colors—a sari of walls surrounding the visage of the core.*
RIGHT: *Detail of pink and green walls, the colors of which were selected after visiting and Indian fabric store.*

This garden reflects separate but interlocking partitas composed at two distinct junctures in time: the rear garden in 1994 and the entry garden in 1999. The topology of the garden was developed collaboratively with our clients to reference a series of historical vignettes, which chronicles distinct spiritual and cultural attitudes of the garden.

This "chance" collaboration in time and space between the client and the artist is required to establish the formal process of creating a distinct garden. By hand, by form, we render in explicit language the reflection (internal) and emulation (external) of the spiritual nature of the garden. This is a garden devoted to the precepts of reflection and revelation within the context of a temperate climate and the gridded formal abstraction of nature—the "suburbs."

In reverse passage through the garden from the internal to the external, one leaves the trapezoidal mediation room (fifty feet in length, twenty-feet wide contracting to one-foot in width) through apertures ascending from one-foot to five-foot openings. The shadow of this trapezoidal room tracks across the shadow plane of decomposed granite flanked by the "American Rose Garden", ebullient with splashes of red, orange, lavender, and white colors. Located directly in front of this floral abundance is the sculptural installation of a linear processional composition of stained wood blocks rotating in form from the cube to the triangle—an allusion to both natural and mathematical processes of nature. Flanking the other side of the shadow plane is a terrace of pink marbleized concrete defined by saffron plaster walls, the reverse of which reveals vibrant chartreuse surfaces enclosing the "orangerie".

OPPOSITE PAGE: *The metaphor of glass reflects the relationship between the manufactured glass surfaces of the architecture and the congealed forms of glass in the land. The metamorphic and refractive properties of glass were selected as an allusion to the historical geologic metamorphosis of the stones of Royanjii; however, we are now in California with a currency of new technologies where rocks are transformed into glass lit by fiberoptics.*
ABOVE: *A sandblasted glass panel forms a translucent entrance to the threshold of the garden.*

Two planar celadon stucco walls define the shift from the decomposed granite court of the shadow plane to a terrace of honed black granite, which extends through the ground plane of the house to the entry garden adjacent to the street. A sole olive tree forms a dappled canopy over this reflective black surface. The leaf color mimics the shade tones of the architecture's glass walls. Planted on either side of this black formal terrace are two balanced planes of lavender bisected by gravel paths, which lead respectively to an herb garden and a fountain of water flowing over a glass disc. Walking past this fountain through the callas to the side garden we use the wheel path constructed to provide both a walk and a surface for the wheelbarrow filled with garden clippings to be wheeled through to the entry garden and the street.

In the entry garden we meter our step to a deliberate slow pace, our body in motion following a narrow sinuous ribbon of black concrete, "The Scholar's Walk", which curves through a plane of green baby's tears. Again, we walk on the rectilinear plane of black granite, which extends from the core of the garden through the house to the entry path ending at the public sidewalk. Punctuating

the monochromatic text of baby's tears glass orbs glowing kryptonite green positioned as allusions to Japanese gardens of contemplation such as Royanji, where the viewer contemplates nature through the abstraction of natural forms. The viewer is extant-exterior to the garden observing the external. The entry threshold of stainless steel and sandblasted glass both defines and deflects the light and shadow of the exterior street—the threshold of intersection between the profane (the external) and the sacred (the internal).

RIGHT: *The principle of kū-tei is investigated through the selection of material and form within the entry garden. The granite entry slab/path is an allusion to the viewing platform—a linear intervention flanked by the monochromatic text of baby's tears and glass gravel. This garden is viewed both in passage and internally from the core of the home.*
FOLLOWING PAGE LEFT: *Black concrete "wheelbarrow" path flanked by callas.*
FOLLOWING PAGE RIGHT: *Reflections on the black concrete "Scholar's Walk" set within a plane of baby's tears.*

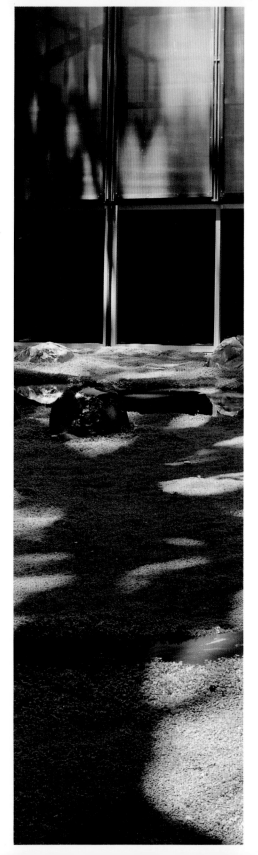

FAR LEFT: *"The orangerie." The mellifluous scent of Seville oranges from potted citrus trees.*
LEFT: *Chartreuse walls of the orangerie, pink concrete terrace, decomposed granite on "the shadow plane" or petanque court, the perception of which depends on whether you are mediating or playing ball.*
BELOW: *Lavender "Goodwin Creek" is bisected by plaster celadon walls, a fruitless olive "Majestic Beauty" overlays the black granite terrace.*
BELOW RIGHT: *A field of lavender flanks the rear of the house. The tonality of the plant's leaves mimic the vertical tones of the architectures, silver, glass and stucco.*

LEFT: *Looking north—"the trapezoidal garden room" lavender gravel from Barstow, California, walls diffused by the roil of bougainvillaea, trumpet vine and red blaze roses.*

RIGHT: *the shadow of the apertures transverse across the shadow plane of the composed granite. This room is created as a monumental* gnomon *which serves as both a resting place and a sculptural form which charts the shadow of the passage of light.*

OPPOSITE PAGE: *Looking south—the form of the room contracts from twenty-feet to the compression of one-foot. Views through the apertures.*

HARLEQUIN GARDEN

"Pay no attention to the man behind the curtain."
—The Wizard of Oz

This south-facing garden located to the right of the entrance to the house is directly adjacent to the elevated dining and family rooms. This installation focuses on the use of theatrical devices. Bisecting lines of a diamond pattern extend the visual length and width of the garden. Oversized, elevated steel planters hold wide brimmed date palms forming an immediate green canopy of intimacy. At the terminus of the garden the placement of mirror strips located at the apex of the steel plates dissolves the perception of the property's actual limits reflecting a garden that exists only in our imagination—calling into question the validity of the visual information we assume to be "real."

There is a balance of both traditional and contemporary gestures within the graphic form of this garden. These acts are revealed in the paving, a classic black and white harlequin pattern bounded by trapezoidal steel planters, the steel screens, the mirrors, and the cast-bronze Italianate fish, spitting water into a surreal clam shell filled with glass cullet. The flounce and drift of Sally Holmes roses, the thick forms date and sago palms and the confetti of perennial blooms envelop these discrete surfaces to create an intimate room for reverie.

ABOVE: *Sally Holmes roses cascade over an edge band of paving turned on its side. The balcony of the first floor overlooks the garden.*
OPPOSITE PAGE: *A cast iron Florentine fish spews water into a chalice of water. A mirror backing reflects the garden amplifying the diagonal pattern of the concrete tiles. Cold rolled steel panels form an impenetrable shoji screen. Mirror strips create the illusion of a garden which extends beyond.*

LEFT: *Trapezoidal cold rolled steel planters with grass, glass cullet, palms and candles.*

RIGHT: *Detail of a* Sansevieria trifasciata *with black and white concrete diamond edge bands.*

OPPOSITE PAGE: *Balconies extend into the garden flanked by raised steel planters of* Phoenix canariensis *to create a "room with a view."*

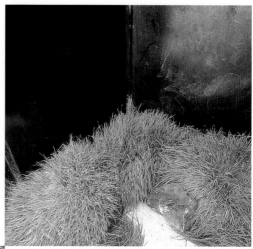

LEFT: *A marble panel is positioned as a site specific installation which alludes to a state of being—antithetical to the reference of this ceremonial marker of passage.*

OPPOSITE PAGE: *The topiary pot garden—a herd of rosemary, thyme, and bay are corralled by the front entrance tethered to the land by feet of clay.*

GOLDFARB GARDEN

Often depicted through the medium of black and white photography, historical gardens lay bare their structures. We can easily trace form and content through this reduction of visual information. I chose to represent this garden in this format for the intrinsic reason of its creation, the "historical" re-creation of a garden. The intent was to extend and expound upon the existing form, a structure of distinctive brick architecture. The creation of a seamless connection between both the existing structure of the 1930s and the garden, created in 1978, was achieved through the verisimilitude of materials, which reflects the text and texture of the site structures.

Within this garden, seemingly traditional in its layout and use of materials, is the placement of a significant device of illusion, front and center, similar to the Harlequin Garden completed in 1998. The use of mirror illuminates and extends the perception of the exact dimensions of the garden. Both gardens are intimate in their scale and urban location. The historical framework of the garden is bisected directly in the center core by the mirror—an illusion and metaphor to imagination and to the question of perception—what is real and what is not real. The introduction of this device is the beginning of an investigation into aspects of coded information within the landscape of man.

LEFT: *Cast iron patinated rails rim the elevated tile terraces. Front and center is a mirror enveloped within the arch of the constructed brick rim walls.*

BELOW: *Cast concrete elevated koi pond. Brick clad metal arches support tile terraces with copper moulding panels.*

OPPOSITE PAGE: *Detail of mirror. Ficus tree hedge. Formal boxwood and herb garden. Handmade copper lights mimic the form of the arch.*

FOLLOWING PAGE LEFT: *Detail of Welsh tile on terrace.*

FOLLOWING PAGE RIGHT: *Handcast spiral staircase produced by Robinson Ironworks.*

BELOW: *New steel sash door with Welsh tile thresholds.*
OPPOSITE PAGE: *Musing on the reflections of the illusory.*

HOTEL KOHJIMACHI KAIKAN

The Garden of Blue Mountains and Green Water

ABOVE: *View from coffee shop*
OPPOSITE PAGE: *Cascade and pond*

There are few places in the city capable of reproducing the sublime effects of Nature. Stands of trees, pools and fountains, and flowerbeds surrounding buildings cannot truly duplicate the wild elements of the natural world. Sprawling urban centers may inspire awe, but they seldom offer a sense of peace or repose.

Hotel Kohjimachi Kaikan, in Chiyoda, Tokyo, is located in just such a harsh environment. It is surrounded by a garden designed to provide the casual visitor with a memorable moment of peace during a short visit. It is a Japanese garden, however, not nature itself. It is a spiritual space designed according to sophisticated Japanese aesthetic principles that evoke and celebrate nature. Such a garden truly is what is needed in the urban environment.

The Kohjimachi Kaikan was designed to contain several small internal garden spaces. They are laid out as terraces, one on the main floor and two on the fourth floor, providing a natural atmosphere for contemplation and revitalization in the chaotic heart of Tokyo. The gardens adhere to the traditional Japanese sense of beauty and the spirit of Zen, to which we applied a modern understanding. This garden would be classified as a work of the Heisei era.

The three small gardens are called Seizan-Ryokusui No Niwa (The Garden of Blue Mountains and Green Water). The vision they convey is one of absolute peacefulness, as if one were deep within the forested mountains.

85

The waterfall garden on the main floor mingles the peaceful, refreshing, and musical sounds of running water. Flowing water is symbolized through the use of gravel in the two gardens on the fourth floor, where the viewer may imagine a running river. This area totally separates the viewer from the urban environment. One is left to meditate in silence on the meaning of such a space, with its harmonic marriage of water and plants. The layering of tree branches and the composition of rocks further imply the endless extension of the space. In Zen this convergence of natural and manmade objects creates an experience that reveals the cosmos and is referred to yohaku, or blankness. It is a moment of opportunity that unites people with nature.

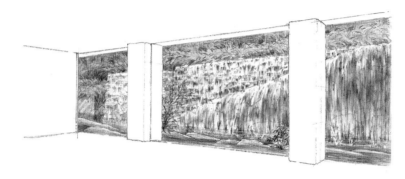

LEFT: *Sketch*
BELOW: *Plan on 1st floor*
OPPOSITE PAGE: *Night view of the cascade and pond*

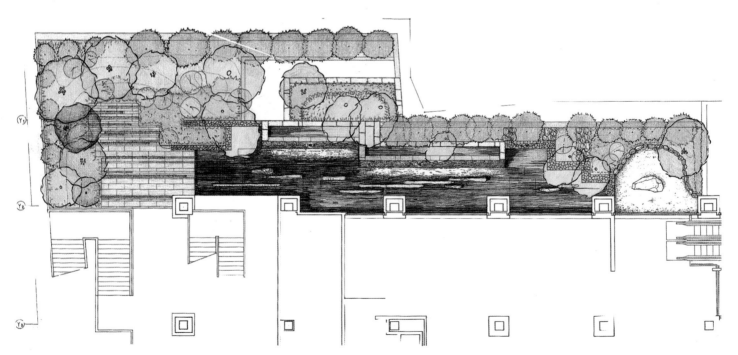

LEFT: *Sketch*
BELOW: *Plan on 4th floor*
OPPOSITE PAGE: *Rock arrangement
and Kohetuji-style bamboo fence*

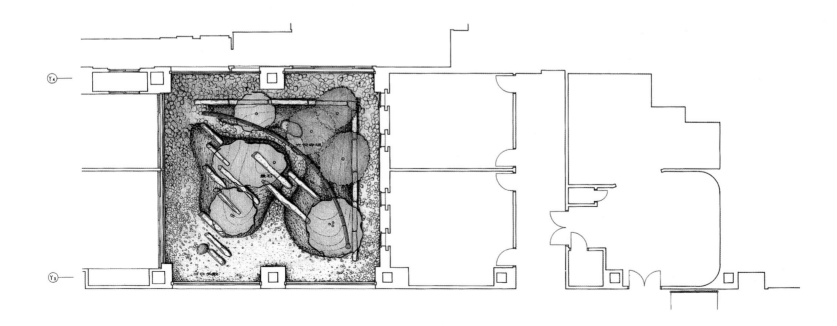

RIGHT: *Second Japanese garden on
fourth floor*
BELOW: *Plan of garden on 4th floor*

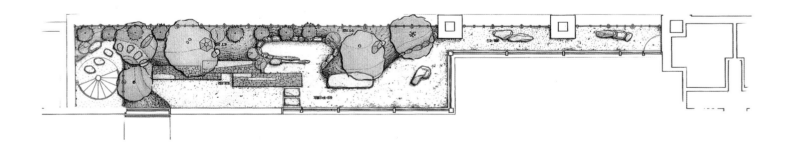

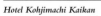

LEFT: *Bamboo fence hiding adjacent buildings*
BELOW LEFT: *Sketch*

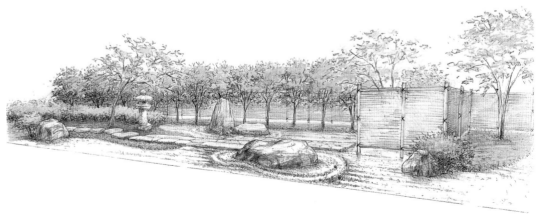

IMABARI KOKUSAI HOTEL

The Garden of a Great Waterfall and Pine Trees

This Japanese garden was inspired by the Setonaikai area in Japan, where Imabari is located. It consists of two distinct gardens. Water is the motif of the main garden, and simplicity is the basis for the Roji-the inner tea garden.★

The combined elements of pond, stream, and waterfalls invent the spirit of the place. White sand implies the sea, and granite rocks represent islands in the sea. The rock is the focus of the design. Three pine trees symbolize an impressive stillness in the landscape. By contrast, running water represents the dynamic element of nature. A steep grade enabled the construction of several waterfalls; the largest one is great enough to be called baku, or great fall, and it produces echoes deep in the body. The contrast of stillness and movement is the key element of this design.

This garden further emphasizes that maintaining a balance between opposing forces-stillness and movement-is an important matter for our existence and well-being. Everyday life is full of activities and restlessness. The motion of the powerful waterfall, combined with the presence of the still pines, seems to calm us and clear our restless, worried minds. This is why I named this garden Bakusyou-tei, "The garden of great waterfall and pine trees."

★Roji is a small garden path setting created for the tea ceremony. Each element is placed according to the rules of tea. The journey through the garden allows the cleansing of oneself before entering the tea house.

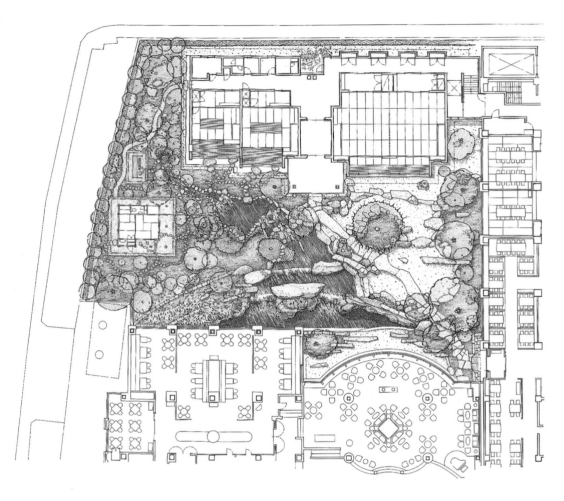

Imabari Kokusai Hotel

ABOVE RIGHT: *Plan*
RIGHT: *Fashioned stone basin*

LEFT: *Garden overlooked from upper level*

FOLLOWING PAGE: *View to the tea house from the Japanese style annex building*

LEFT: *View from "Nijiriguchi" (miniature entrance to the tea house)*
OPPOSITE PAGE: *Around the tea house*

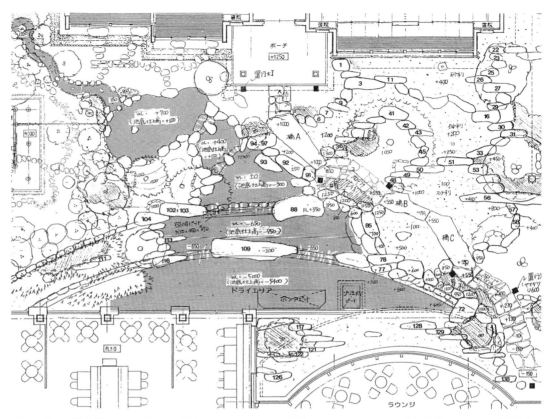

ABOVE RIGHT: *Plan for the layout of rocks*

RIGHT: *View from the lounge*

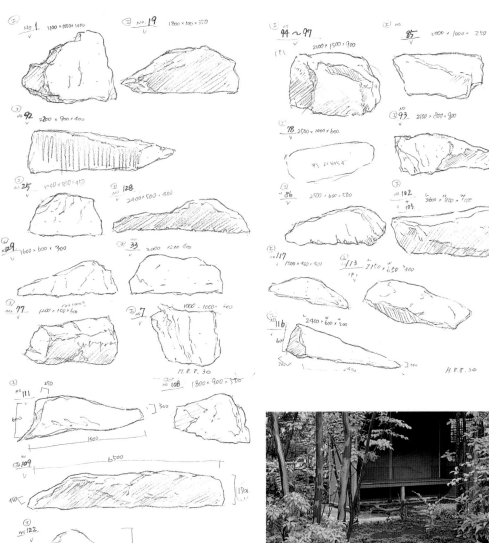

ABOVE LEFT: *Sketch of rocks at the time of selection*
LEFT: *View to the "Machiai"*

HANOURA INFORMATION/ CULTURE CENTER

The Garden of Neither More Nor Less

The main feature of this garden is a large body of water surrounded by pine trees. The garden is called, Fuzou-fumetsu to reflect an attitude of facing facts as they are. This attitude is metaphorically expressed in a Chinese legend depicting a carp absorbed in an attempt to climb a waterfall. The carp's virtuous fight moves and reminds us to encounter reality despite earthly desires. The waterfall is called Ryu-mon-baku (the dragon gate of strong waterfall). The process of self-examination or of enduring hardship to gain success is called, To-ryu-mon (to pass through the dragon gate). It is believed that one becomes able to see truths and accept everything undisguised when one has purely confronted difficulties. The real value of a thing does not increase nor decrease according to its contemporary reputation. The spirit of Fuzou-fumetsu (neither more nor less) involves recognizing the significance of being. By concentrated viewing one's spirit will unite with the garden. I believe this is the moment that one feels purified and at absolute peace. The composition of stones in the middle of the garden, called Sanzon-seki, is derived from the Buddhist trinity symbolizing the tranquility of the place.

LEFT: *Plan*
BELOW: *Sketch for pine tree*
OPPOSITE PAGE: *Picture window of the library*

LEFT AND OPPOSITE PAGE: *Night view*

LEFT: *Stone lantern and Japanese apricot tree*
OPPOSITE PAGE: *Stepping stones over the pond and water basin*

KAGAWA PREFECTURAL LIBRARY

The Garden where Fresh Winds Blow In and Blow Away

ABOVE: *Chinese Elm and chiseled rocks*
OPPOSITE PAGE: *Chiseled rocks*

Originally this site was used as an airport runway. For many years, the memories, sorrows, and hopes of many people passed through this place. The site was destined to be a powerful place to contemplate the blowing winds and to cultivate a peaceful mind.

An airport-a place of coming and going, of moving into and returning from the heavens-is a perfect site for contemplating the past and dreaming about the future. The goal here was to design the place as a heavenly place, where trees, the sky, and singing birds gently surrounded everything. People who experience the breath of the wind here will never lose their way. This sentiment is represented by its name: Seifuu Kyorai No Niwa (The garden where fresh winds blow in and blow away).

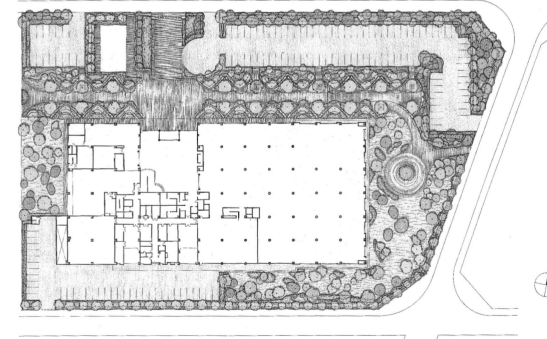

LEFT: *Chinese Elm and stainless circle bench*

BELOW: *Plan*

OPPOSITE PAGE: *Tulip trees and Japanese andromeda planted along site*

RIGHT: *Trees with circular curbing*

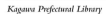

LEFT: *Picture window from the library*
BELOW: *Image sketch*

LEFT: *Impressive rocks*
BELOW: *Sketch for designed rocks*
OPPOSITE PAGE: *Placed rocks*

CANADIAN MUSEUM
OF CIVILIZATION

The Garden for Harmonious Relationship with Respect

ABOVE: *Stepping stones*
OPPOSITE PAGE: *Waterfall rock arrangement*

This traditional Japanese Zen Garden is located on a public terrace rooftop. It is called, Wakei No Niwa, which, roughly translated, means to understand and respect all cultures-their history, spirit, and people-which leads to cultural harmony. The garden design features an extensive gravel raked garden, a dry "waterfall," and a stone bridge. All materials used in this garden were selected in the hills surrounding the region. The dry waterfall is the focus of the garden and is the symbolic source of Japanese influence.

The garden is oriented toward visitors as they arrive at the place of honor: a special assembly area located in the garden. An axis was formed in a gathering area inside the museum, and it leads to the garden, then extends over the waterfall, across the Ottawa River, and on to the Japanese Embassy. The dry stream wraps around the area, and appears to flow through the windows of the museum's Collections/Administration building, symbolizing the infusion of Japanese culture in Canadian culture.

This garden serves as a museum display as well as being part of the museum's total landscape design. Although it appears complete, this is only the first phase of the project. The next phase of construction will complete the lower level entry to the garden and a planned upper level area above the main garden, which will serve several important functions.

The garden on the upper level is designed to reinforce the connection with the Japanese Embassy across the Ottawa River, and it is a splendid place to view the garden from another perspective. It will be adorned with a natural rock carved into a bench, which will unite the traditional Zen garden with the contemporary expression of Zen.

It is crucial in building such a sparse design to listen to the "conversation" among all the materials-such as the plants and stones-as well as to be aware of the spaces between objects. Both the creator of a Zen garden and the viewer should be "at one" with the garden when they regard it. Our attempt was to help the museum's visitors better understand themselves and their landscape through this garden.

RIGHT: *Plan*

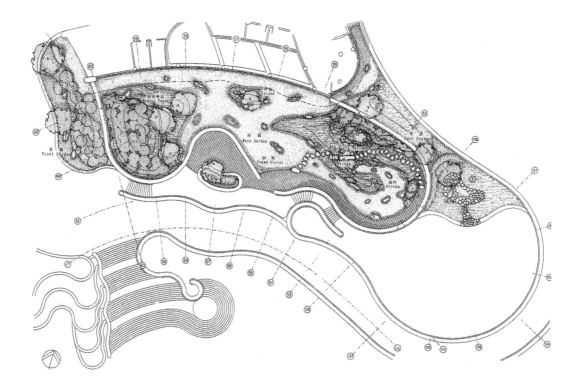

LEFT: *The garden was designed with the building's shape in mind.*

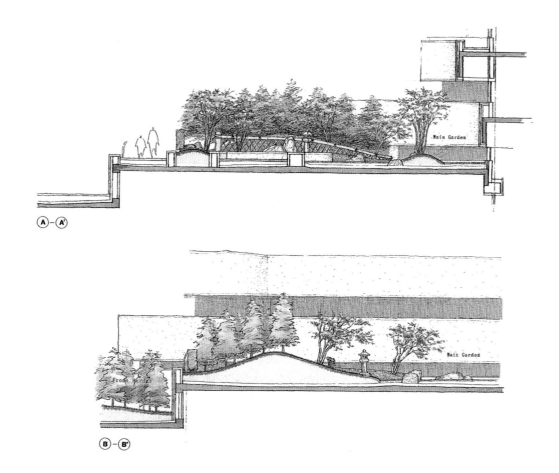

A – A'

B – B'

ABOVE RIGHT: *Section*
RIGHT: *Sketch*

C – C'

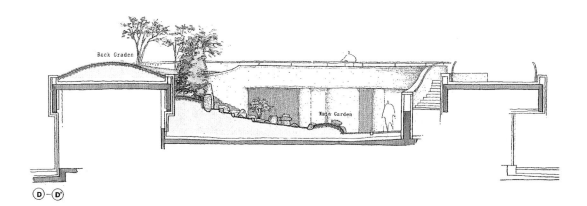

D – D'

DRY WATER FALL AND STREAM

ABOVE LEFT: *Section*
LEFT: *Sketch*

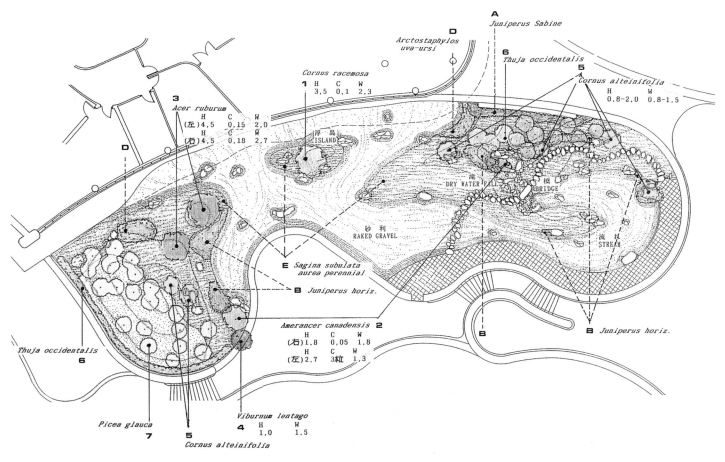

A Juniperus Sabine

D

Arctostaphylos
uva-ursi

Thuja occidentalis

6

5

Cornus racemosa
1 H   C   W
   3,5 0,1 2,3

Cornus alteinifolia
H   W
0,8-2,0   0,8-1,5

3

Acer ruburum
      H   C   W
(左) 4,5 0,15 2,0
      H   C   W
(右) 4,5 0,18 2,7

D

浮島
ISLAND

滝
DRY WATER FALL

橋
BRIDGE

砂利
RAKED GRAVEL

流れ
STREAM

E Sagina subulata
   aurea perennial

B Juniperus horiz.

B Juniperus horiz.

Amerancer canadensis 2
      H   C   W
(右) 1,8 0,05 1,8
      H   C   W
(左) 2,7 3杜   1,3

B

Thuja occidentalis
6

Viburnum lentago
4 H   W
   1,0   1,5

Picea glauca
7

5

Cornus alteinifolia

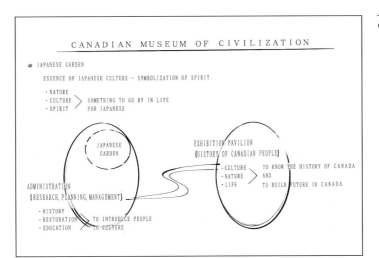

CANADIAN MUSEUM OF CIVILIZATION

⊘ JAPANESE GARDEN

ESSENCE OF JAPANESE CULTURE = SYMBOLIZATION OF SPIRIT

· NATURE
· CULTURE   ⟩ SOMETHING TO GO BY IN LIFE
· SPIRIT   FOR JAPANESE

JAPANESE
GARDEN

EXHIBITION PAVILION
(HISTORY OF CANADIAN PEOPLE)

· CULTURE   TO KNOW THE HISTORY OF CANADA
· NATURE   AND
· LIFE   TO BUILD FUTURE IN CANADA

ADMINISTRATION
[RESEARCH, PLANNING, MANAGEMENT]

· HISTORY
· RESTORATION → TO INTRODUCE PEOPLE
· EDUCATION   TO CULTURE

Canadian Museum of Civilization

ABOVE RIGHT: *Conceptual charts*
RIGHT: *Section*
OPPOSITE PAGE TOP: *Finished water-fall rock arrangement*
OPPOSITE PAGE BOTTOM: *Planting plan*

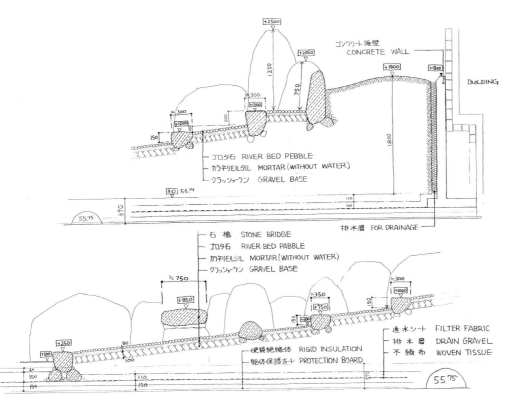

ゴンクリート擁壁 CONCRETE WALL

BUILDING

ゴロタ石 RIVER BED PEBBLE
カラネリモルタル MORTAR (WITHOUT WATER)
クラッシャーラン GRAVEL BASE

排水層 FOR DRAINAGE

石 橋 STONE BRIDGE
ゴロタ石 RIVER BED PABBLE
カラネリモルタル MORTAR (WITHOUT WATER)
クラッシャーラン GRAVEL BASE

透水シート FILTER FABRIC
排水層 DRAIN GRAVEL
不織布 WOVEN TISSUE

硬質絶縁体 RIGID INSULATION
躯体保護ボード PROTECTION BOARD

125

THE UNIVERSITY OF BRITISH COLUMBIA

Renovation of the Nitobe Garden

ABOVE: *Water flows to the pond*
OPPOSITE PAGE: *Wooden bridge leading onto the island*

This was a major project to restore and renovate gardens that were laid out in 1960, as a memorial to the scholar and educator, Inazo Nitobe, who died while visiting British Columbia. The original plan was designed by Kannosuke Mori. Over the years the gardens had been changed considerably, and the concepts behind its design were no longer discernible. Indeed, it would have been impossible to renovate it at all without removing such impediments as the concrete coating that was sprayed over the original shoreline stonework in 1974 to prevent it from leaking.

The scheme to renovate these gardens was developed after considering what Mori himself would have done had he been alive today. We also investigated the things he wanted to do during the gardens' construction but for some reason was unable to accomplish. We were able to return the original island to the pond, restore the shoreline stonework, and add new beaches. The tea house and garden were also updated and restored. To help shut out the noise of traffic, we constructed a traditional Japanese mud wall around the entire garden. Finally, a pathway and entry gate were constructed to define and locate the gardens.

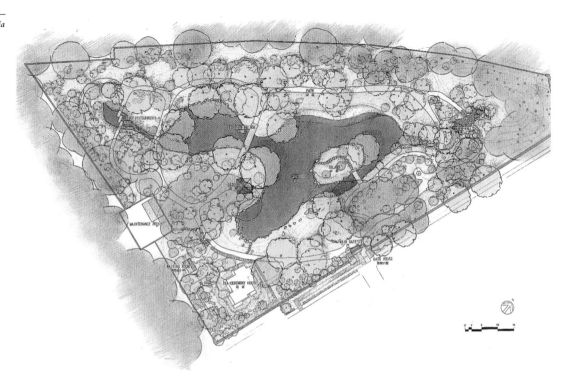

ABOVE: *Plan*

RIGHT: *Rock arrangement at the ponds edge*

OPPOSITE PAGE: *Another bridge*

PREVIOUS PAGE: *Renovated garden*

ABOVE RIGHT: *Newly constructed
main gate*
RIGHT: *Detail of main gate*

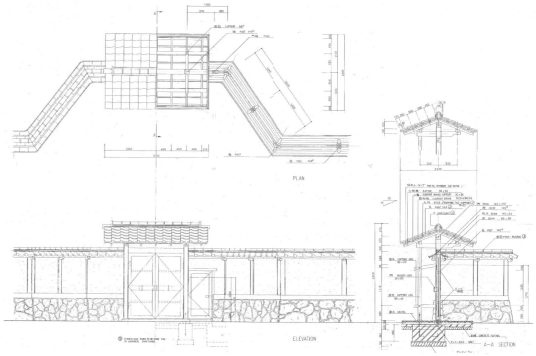

LEFT: *Newly constructed "Tsuijibei" wall and stone path*

ABOVE RIGHT: *Overlooking tea house from "Machiai"*

ABOVE FAR RIGHT: *Renovated tea garden*

RIGHT: *Path to the tea house*

ABOVE LEFT: *Sketch (rock arrangement for waterfall)*
LEFT: *Water cascades into the pond*

NATIONAL RESEARCH INSTITUTE FOR METALS, SCIENCE AND TECHNOLOGY AGENCY

The Plaza of Whiteness Refined by Natural Power

ABOVE: *Group of rocks and pebbled stream*
OPPOSITE PAGE: *Overall view*

The theme of this garden came naturally after a visit to the site. What first struck me was the notion of purity, which is one of the most important and difficult things for people to attain. Scientists working here needed a pure mind to perform. The garden had to be a place where the symbol of purity existed.

In addition, the site called to mind the relationship between man and metal during the American Gold Rush. During that time, thousands of people journeyed into the mountains to pursue their dream. What they found was a dry, inhospitable range of craggy mountains sparsely dotted with scrub trees and grasses. In the valleys there were dry twisting river beds and little water.

The prospectors, therefore, were not only searching for gold; they were also looking for water to relieve their weary bodies. Often they would meet at a place where there was a spring. This was where they found the hope and energy to face another day's toil.

Prospectors worked alone digging and panning for ore. In similar fashion, researchers at this institute also work alone. So despite the differences between a mine and a research laboratory, prospectors and researchers have in common the fact that their work is often a solitary battle. By understanding this similarity, we were able to make the plaza a place where isolated and solitary researchers might be rejuvenated.

What emerged was a dry, chalky landscape scattered with hard, sharp stones. Large stones laid toward the building represent human lives. The stones are washed by rain and polished by the gritty winds, until they are gradually purified and bleached. Man's spirit also is purified by experiencing harsh circumstances.

White is the symbol of purity and of Buddha's heart. In Zen philosophy, the tremendous power of nature revitalizes the weary mind and returns it to its original whiteness. This acetic practice is called byakuren, through which human beings may receive the power of nature and reclaim their pure spirit, in the way that stones are bleached by the sun. The plaza of whiteness refined by natural power is thus a place for the research scientist to rediscover the clarity of his or her goals, direction, and dreams.

RIGHT: *Plan*
OPPOSITE PAGE: *Stone bridge with stepping stones*

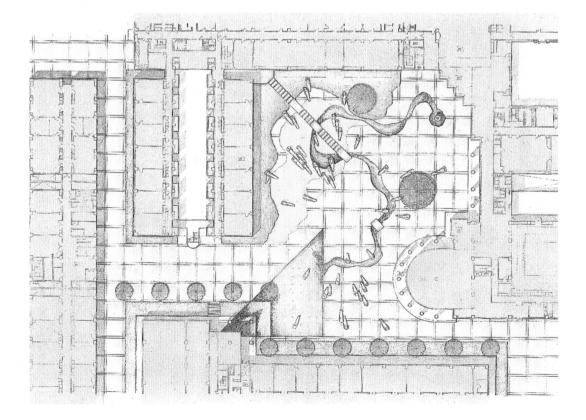

ABOVE RIGHT: *Seen from the entrance hall*

RIGHT: *Perspective*

OPPOSITE PAGE: *Night view*

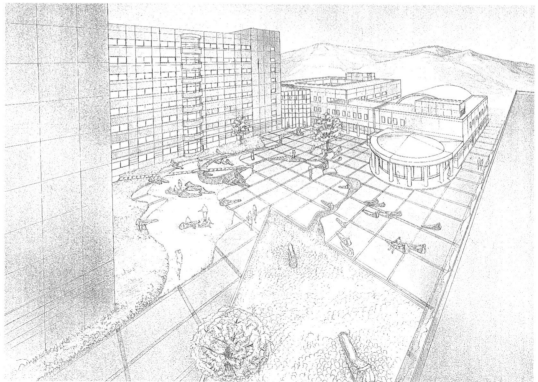

ABOVE RIGHT: *Mist covers the placed rocks*

RIGHT: *The chiseled rocks contrast sharply with the symmetrical paving*

ABOVE LEFT: *Chiseled rock symbolically placed*
LEFT: *Group of rocks placed beside mist*

NIIGATA PREFECTURAL MUSEUM OF MODERN ART

Unity of Earth and Sky

A long-term ambition has been to design a place where people can be absorbed in a magnificent landscape and recognize themselves as part of nature. To produce this, a huge open space was needed. The grounds surrounding the site of the Niigata Prefectural Museum of Modern Art afforded the ideal conditions for such a project. Two-thirds of the building is located underground, so the impression is that it has emerged naturally out of the earth. The Shinano River runs parallel to the site. Standing on the hilltop, with the boundless sky above and the vast, flowing Shinano River below, the view extends towards a peaceful countryside into the horizon. This is a space that enables one to experience the universe.

Tenchi ittai refers to the state of not discriminating among earth, sky, and man. When one realizes that man is a small part of such a vast relationship, we recognize the great power that daily affects our existence. Experiencing tenchi ittai space invokes our thankfulness for our existence. The garden is designed to summon this state into the hearts of the many people who will visit this museum.

Using the Shinano River as a starting point to determine ways in which man can live in harmony with nature, we attempted to develop the design along the two metaphorical axes of time and space.

The museum itself stands at the intersection of the city and nature, which the river represents. Its flow symbolizes not only the passage of time from the past through the present and into the future, but alternatively, its recursive movement once more to the past. In the physical world time moves forward. Within the spiritual world it is possible to retrace one's steps into the past through memories. These two flows of time were considered as we laid out the garden.

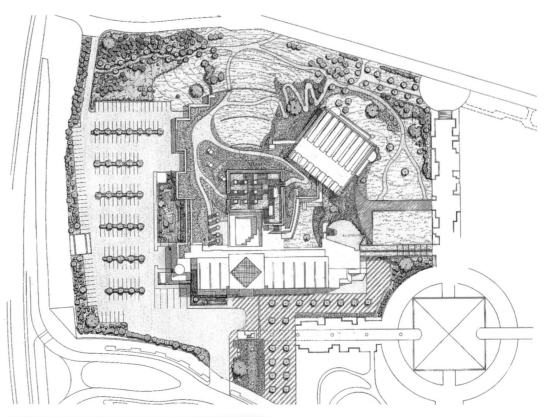

ABOVE RIGHT: *Plan*

RIGHT: *Continuous thread-like white cascade and decorative columns*

ABOVE LEFT: *Front elevation of the museum at night*

LEFT: *Movement of water seen from the lobby*

FOLLOWING PAGES: *Landscaped roof of the museum*

Niigata Museum of Modern Art

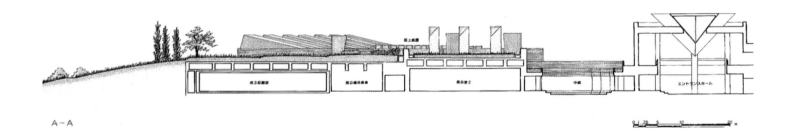

A－A

B－B

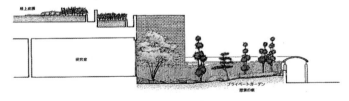

C－C

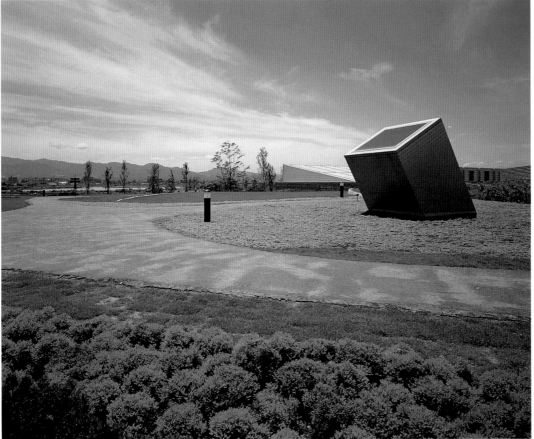

ABOVE LEFT: *Pond and pavement*
ABOVE RIGHT: *Museum seen from the south*
RIGHT: *Skylight tower*
OPPOSITE PAGE TOP: *Path on the roof*
OPPOSITE PAGE BOTTOM: *Sections*

DENENCHOFU PARK CONDOMINIUM

Compatibility

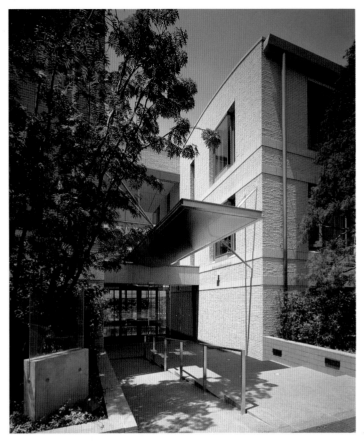

This building is located on a hillside covered with rich greenery in one of the most prestigious residential neighborhoods of Tokyo. The western edge of the site was a steep woodland slope. Within the woods a majestic Japanese red pine was dominant. It looked like the master of the land, inheriting its history and governing the site.

The theme for designing the site is yu-wa, or compatibility. This describes the attempt to create a harmonious relationship between the site and its surroundings, the new building the natural topography that surrounds it.

The site's beautiful existing trees are reflected in the four imperatives of the design. The first was to provide lush vegetation along the street front. Second was to preserve as many existing trees as possible. The third was to transplant any trees that lay in the path of construction. The fourth was to ensure that the architectural elements faded into the greenery.

153

An ornamental wall plays an important role in providing a special experience of the place. It extends from the building and follows the grade. The wall steps to the lower level where a cozy terrace, hidden from view, provides just enough space for an intimate bench. The view from here is dominated by the large Japanese pine.

The building is connected to the site by rocks that cover the surface of the slope around the pine tree. By blending the rough texture and the architectural arrangement, a space was created where a harmonious relationship between man and nature could develop in a severely limited urban space. Today in Tokyo a comforting sitting area under a mature tree's canopy is indeed a rarity. The condominium provides an experience seldom enjoyed in today's Tokyo.

RIGHT: *Plan*

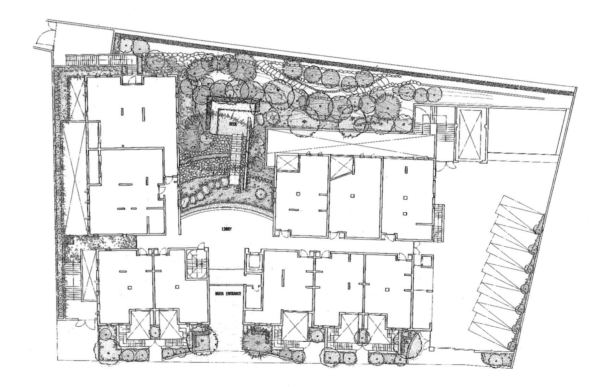

LEFT: *Existing big red pine tree creating the shade to the steps*

Denenchofu Park Condominium

ABOVE: *Sketch for terrace*
RIGHT: *Ornamental wall, steps, and terrace*

LEFT: *Utilizing existing stepping stones*

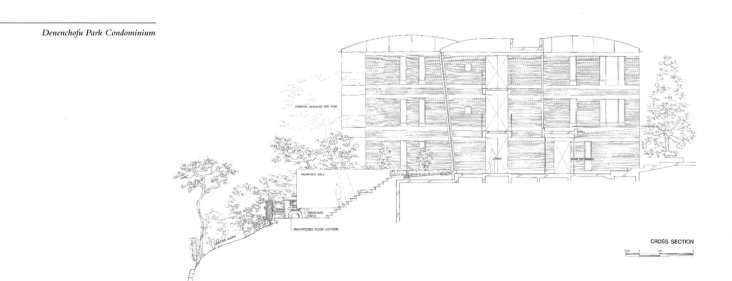

CROSS SECTION

ABOVE RIGHT: *Section*
RIGHT: *Planting plan for transferred and preserved trees*

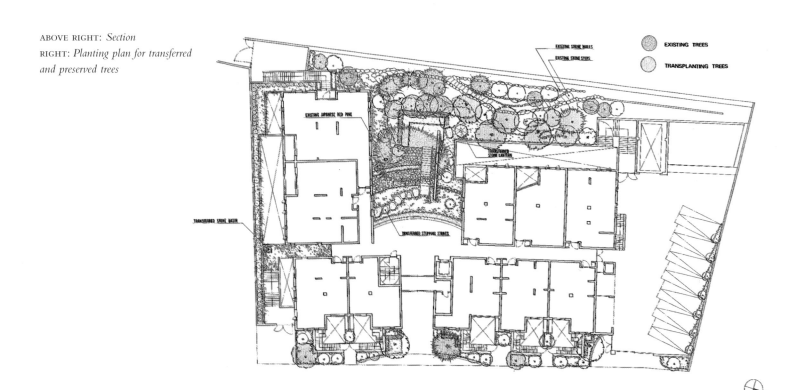

EXISTING TREES

TRANSPLANTING TREES

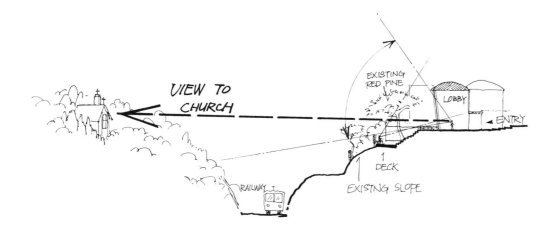

VIEW TO CHURCH

EXISTING RED PINE

LOBBY

ENTRY

1 DECK

EXISTING SLOPE

RAILWAY

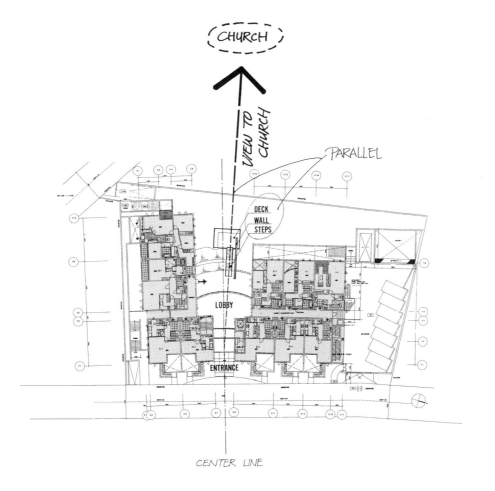

CHURCH

VIEW TO CHURCH

PARALLEL

DECK WALL STEPS

LOBBY

ENTRANCE

CENTER LINE

LETHAM GRANGE HOTEL AND GOLF COURSE

Stones of Good Fortune

ABOVE: *Placed rock in one with nature*
OPPOSITE PAGE: *Placed rocks*

In this project, I "blow spirits" into the stones that have slept deep within the bowels of the earth for millennia. These stones, excavated from a quarry in Aberdeen, Scotland, were destined to be crushed for road fill. Yet, for the sixty-six stones selected from the huge quarry, my visit changed their destiny. When I create a stone composition, I first gaze into the "spirit" of each stone to learn and memorize its character. This is the beginning of many conversations I hold with the stones. Then I set them with great care to liberate their characteristics (which I call ishi gokoro, or "the heart of the stone") as much as possible.

The stones are truly happy to cooperate with me in my work. Especially the stones used in this project, for now they rest in the most beautiful areas on the golf course, perhaps for eternity. When visitors see or touch the stones, they will witness their lives in the long history and good fortune of the stones. Providing an opportunity for people to pursue the spirit of Zen and to think about their own life is one of my life's great pleasures.

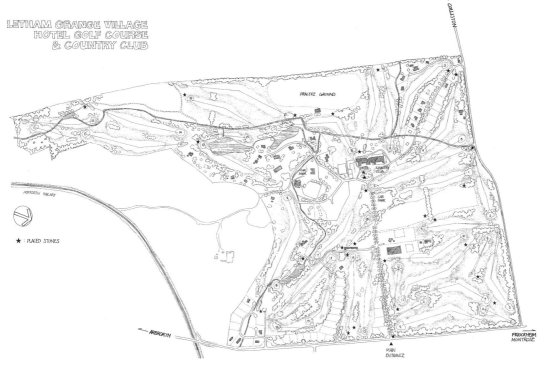

LETHAM GRANGE VILLAGE
HOTEL GOLF COURSE
& COUNTRY CLUB

PRACTICE GROUND

COLLISTON

ABERDEEN RAILWAY

★ : PLACED STONES

ARBROATH

MAIN ENTRANCE

FRIOCKHEIM MONTROSE

ABOVE: *Plan*
LEFT: *Symbolically placed rock*
OPPOSITE PAGE: *Symbolically placed rock*

Letham Grange Hotel and Golf Course

ABOVE RIGHT: *Placed rocks in front of the hotel*

RIGHT: *Supervising placement of rocks*

NO2 + NO4 + NO7   IN FRONT OF HOTEL

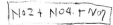

NO3 + NO5   ENTRANCE

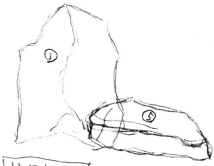

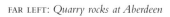

LEFT: *Sketch for rocks*
FAR LEFT: *Quarry rocks at Aberdeen*

NO12 + NO10

MICHAEL BALSTON
MANOR FARM HOUSE

The garden at my home in Wiltshire is the one that has taught me the most about the craft of gardening. Since 1983 I have learned how to grow my own plants in a relatively large garden over a long period of time where I have sole control. I now understand so much more about the business of garden management, how to encourage and control growth, how to direct labor, about the use of chemicals and machinery. There is only a certain amount that you can learn from courses, text books or other people's gardens. In your own you live with your mistakes or you root them out and start again. It has also taught me more about exploiting location and the environmental aspects of the Genius of the Place. The shelter of walls and southerly elevations of the building may appear obvious, but there are surprising subtleties that can seldom be discovered by a visiting designer. Some things are only apparent after constant observation.

When I started on our family garden, I was more architect than gardener. More concerned with space and geometry, I wanted to control the planting so that it rigidly reinforced the organizing principles of the garden. Now I am more relaxed about the planting and I realize that the organizing thrust of the design, together with its interlocking spaces, is so strong that almost anything can happen in the planting. This is just as well as I am now keenly interested in chance—the things in gardens that happen by themselves. Seed being blown about into unplanned places can produce some felicitous harmonies or indeed challenging contrasts. The odd bit of disease can produce a host of intriguing opportunities. I conclude that Fate should be a gardener's friend. And the interplay between chance and design is pretty exciting.

ABOVE: *Sculpture is an important part of the garden. This stone apple is located under an apple tree in the orchard.*

The garden's layout is determined by an axis through front and back doors of the house up into the walled garden and field beyond. At the southerly end, close to where my office is now located, we have put a focal urn of my own design, on a pedestal—all pretty traditional, but which suits the essentially eighteenth century farm house. At the northerly end of the axis is a conical mount clad in box and with a spiral path winding round. This is a rather more modern response though still an idea that has been around for the last 5,000 years, at least in Wiltshire although this was only created in 1990, I knew in 1983 that a mount would be an essential part of the composition. Off the central axis are arranged smaller spaces that all have their own special character, exhibiting different colors and textures.

The garden divides into five major themes. The front is relatively formal with pleached hornbeams round a rectangular croquet lawn and a box and peony parterre in the front of the house. While the box has grown steadily, the infilling has gone through many evolutions on account of the particularly difficult growing environment half under the canopy of an enormous *Quercus ilex*.

To the rear is the walled garden. On our arrival in 1983 there were a few old apple trees and a ramshackle shed in this space. We removed the shed and created a stone paved courtyard at the rear of the house that makes a wonderfully protected outdoor dining room on sunny days. This leads up steps to an oval lawn followed by a rectangular lawn and then to the still unfinished shell house that makes a gateway from the walled garden into the kitchen garden. The walled garden is planted with small trees, shrubs, including roses and some herbaceous material and underplanted with spring bulbs. It is far from complete, continuing to evolve and my long-term plan has water and stone in place of the rectangular lawn in front of the shell house.

The third area is the kitchen garden, originally carved out of the southern end of the field. This is not large but seems to supply an almost inexhaustible quantity of vegetables, far more than our actual requirements. It is enclosed by the remains of the mud wall and the thorn hedge and is now twice its original size thanks to a splendid gale in 1990 that blew over a poplar inconsiderately growing in the western half of the garden.

Beyond is the fourth section, the field that contains the mount and a pond. As I write it is foaming with cow parsley, punctuated liberally with blue *Camassia*. Growing up through are vestigial hay meadow grasses, dogstail, cocksfoot, timothy, bents and so on. I let the grass grow on until late July or early August when it gets cut. There are then a couple more cuts, weather permitting, in the autumn before the emergence of the *Colchicums* and *Crocus speciosus*. During spring and summer, paths are cut through the growing grass, which is liberally studded with spring bulbs and summer flowers. The herb layer swirls through a collection of trees that I planted in the 1980s that are now up to 30 feet high in some cases. This is perhaps my favorite part of the garden, where almost all is left to chance.

ABOVE: *These pyramids are for climbing roses and clematis. They provide a focal contrast to the foliage and gave instant height to the garden when it was new.*

The fifth section is occupied by a tennis court and herbaceous border located on ground acquired in 1996. I was determined to make a court that could form a focal space in the garden instead of being tucked away behind a hedge. So we levelled the area, built the court and surrounded it with an oak cloister that is now beginning to make a stout frame for climbing plants. Instead of the more usual chain-link fence, we used a fine nylon net that is almost invisible against the stout oak columns supporting it. Along one side is a mixed border, supported by background shrubs such as *Viburnum*, *Buddleia*, *Sambucus*, *Photinia* and punctuated in the foreground by large clumps of *Cortaderia*, *Miscanthus* and other grasses. On the opposite side is an orchard on an enclosing bank.

I am grievously short of time in the garden at the moment, being too much occupied with other people's gardens, but sooner or later I will spend more there, and experiment and learn more about plants. Perhaps, too, I will overlay the basic design with new ideas in modern materials, demonstrating the multi-layered nature of an evolving garden. Gardening is a temporal art as well as a spatial one, and I look forward to continuing change.

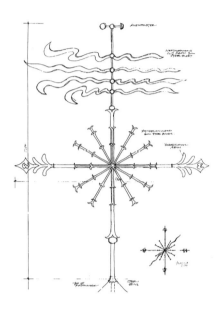

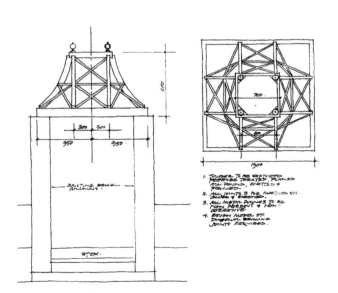

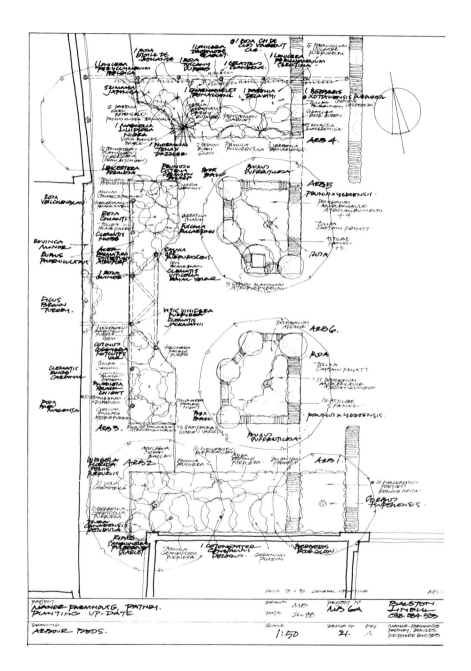

ABOVE: *The shell house and kitchen garden as seen over cow parsley from the mount.*

LEFT: *The central axis through the shell house and kitchen garden looking up towards the field. The succession of spaces leads the eye through to the field.*

OPPOSITE PAGE, CLOCKWISE FROM TOP LEFT: *Sketch for weather vane; partial garden plan; sketch for rose arbor.*

ABOVE: *A paving detail from the shell house created by the gardener Rod Gale.*

LEFT: *The front of the house is swathed with wisteria and roses and overlooks a formal layout of box and santolina.*

OPPOSITE PAGE: *A view through to the oval lawn from the vine clad arbor with* Helleborus x sternii *and* Daphne pontica *in the gap.*

ABOVE: *A sitting area in the walled garden in spring with Tulip Magier and Angelique performing wonderfully.*
RIGHT: *A temporary wild flower area on a recently disturbed bank near the tennis court.*
OPPOSITE PAGE: *The new border along the edge of the tennis court. The plinths are left over from a flower show and flank a sitting area.*

LITTLE MALVERN COURT

ABOVE: *View of the south—the front of the house. The oldest timber-framed part is on the right with the great lime tree opposite.*
OPPOSITE PAGE: *A view towards Hansom's tower from the brick garden. The box-defined bed is filled with bulbs and annuals.*

My earliest long-term relationship with a site began at Little Malvern Court, a large house in the Malvern hills with long views over the Severn Valley towards the Cotswolds. I continued this job from my former partnership with fellow garden designer Arabella Lennox-Boyd. By 1983 Arabella and I had got the bones of the job planned, so from then on I was largely concerned with detailed planning, construction and planting, planning the next phases and then management.

It was really to Arabella Lennox-Boyd that I owed my introduction to gardens. As a landscape architect, I had originally worked on large-scale civic projects with my mentors Hugh Morris and Maurice Lee of Robert Matthew Johnson-Marshall and Partners, a large firm of architects, engineers and planners. Arabella and I joined forces in 1978 and we worked together until 1983 when I moved to Wiltshire. Her practice provided a novel opportunity for me to work for private clients and to become more horticultural. This partly precipitated my departure to the country to get more hands-on experience in my own garden. She had a good eye and a sure touch as well as being an inspiring companion and I learned much during my time with her.

ABOVE: *Circular steps provide access through the retaining wall and allow views from the library down to the lake.*
OPPOSITE PAGE, FAR RIGHT: *Design for plant training wires.*
OPPOSITE PAGE, RIGHT: *Garden plan.*

The house is medieval in foundation and of some literary significance since here is where William Langland wrote his allegorical poem *Piers Plowman* in about 1370. It was much altered since its monastic days, particularly by Joseph Hanson, of horse drawn cab fame, for in the nineteenth century, he completely remodeled the northern end. In 1983, there was a particularly barren sweep of lawn around the building and a magnificent lime tree on the south-east corner. There was a substantial pond, probably a monastic fish pond in origin, though recently altered. I was intrigued to unravel the history, and archival research turned up evidence of a chain of ponds. As the existing pond sat uncomfortably on the hillside, we restored the ponds to their original levels with weirs between them with an elm bridge across. At the changes in level we planted banks of shrubs and herbaceous plants with aquatics and marginals nearby in the water.

With level platforms created by a major new retaining wall, a traditional compartmented layout evolved around the house enclosed by yew hedges, pear espaliers and pleached limes. To the north was a garden of old-fashioned roses supplemented with Chinese junipers, hydrangeas and lots of bulbs for the spring. On a key junction of the paths a timber arbor made a focus that looks spectacular festooned in white climbing roses. In time, I extended the gardens south around the old Priory church and north to the spring, where the main water supply to the lake enters. There a bowl was scooped out of the side of the hill and large rocks brought in to create a tumble of stone with the water running through into the top pond.

This was a germinal work for me and I have been involved there now for nearly twenty years. I have learned much through the kindness of my clients and collaborators in the development of this garden.

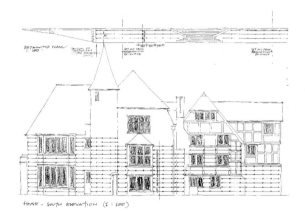

HOUSE - SOUTH ELEVATION (1 : 100)

LITTLE
MALVERN
COURT
WORCESTERSHIRE

GARDEN PLAN

SCALE 1 : 500

CLOCKWISE FROM TOP LEFT: *The lower border below the retaining wall that separates the upper garden from the lawns to the south; the cascade flows southward over timber sleepers with clay between, towards the second and third pond; brick garden with box and yew hedges that give definition in the winter when bulbs and annuals are not evident.*

OPPOSITE PAGE: *Umbrellas of* Prunus 'Ukon' *with trimmed yew hedges beyond.*

ABOVE: *Upper lake and lawn looking across towards the Priory church.*
LEFT: *View along the upper lake towards the south.*
OPPOSITE PAGE: *The lower pond and cascades were created on the site of a former pond, long filled in, to link the waterworks from the spring through the lakes down to Welland.*

JANNAWAYS

One of my earliest jobs having established my own in practice 1983, was executed for Christopher and Sharon Sharples at their London house. They responded well to my ideas and seemed to like the way I went about things. So when they acquired Jannaways, not the most prepossessing of 1930's suntrap houses and deeply overshadowed by vast trees that blocked out both morning and afternoon sun, they kindly asked me to try and help them sort out the immediate problems as well as to plan for the future.

Close to a little tributary of the River Lambourn, the house sits on a chalk slope running down to the stream. With clay at the bottom, boggy areas of peat had formed, making much of the garden extremely wet and virtually unusable. I, therefore, proposed turning most of the garden into a lake—a proposal that my clients bravely acceded to. We could use the spoil from the lake to create a grass terrace for croquet and party marquees—the only flat area on the whole site, apart from the terraces outside the house.

The lake eventually comprised about a third of the garden. The flow of ground water was sufficient to keep it always full and it has become the focus of the garden. At the same time, we built a stone terrace following the line of the house, with two arms projecting out towards tile-roofed, open-sided pavilions overlooking the water. The arms embrace a lower terrace, also in stone, laced through with a brick pattern that picks up the geometry of the building. The idea was to extend the house outward, creating an open-sided outdoor court. This completely transformed the appearance of the original structure making something spacious and elegant out of an otherwise somewhat pedestrian elevation.

All this was part of a longer term development plan that determined spaces for a tennis court, a swimming pool and a kitchen garden, among other things. Although none of these became reality for some time, a strategy for the whole site meant that the work could be carried out in the future as part of a coherent design. Advance planting of trees and hedges ensured that the site structure matured even though the detailed planting came later.

The planting needed to suit the varied conditions ranging from the boggy lower ground to dry shallow chalk on the north side of the house. We·planted many native trees that have prospered and ornamentals trees such as *Pterocarya* on the lake edge, *Betula jacque-montii*, *Liriodendron* and *Metasequoia*. Shrubs were chosen for season and color, though by this time I was beginning to appreciate more the value of texture, which was important in the large areas of marginal planting.

A good relationship developed with an enlightened client so that the work contin-ues—even this year, (2000) we completed steps on the north side that were first mooted back in 1985. A successful garden should work well at a personal level as well as at an aes-thetic and technical level.

FAR RIGHT: *A fountain at the end of the upper terrace.*
RIGHT: *Large seats are useful focal points. This one is in the middle of one side of the lower terrace.*
BELOW: *Plan for ornamental pool and seating area.*
OPPOSITE PAGE: *Garden plan.*

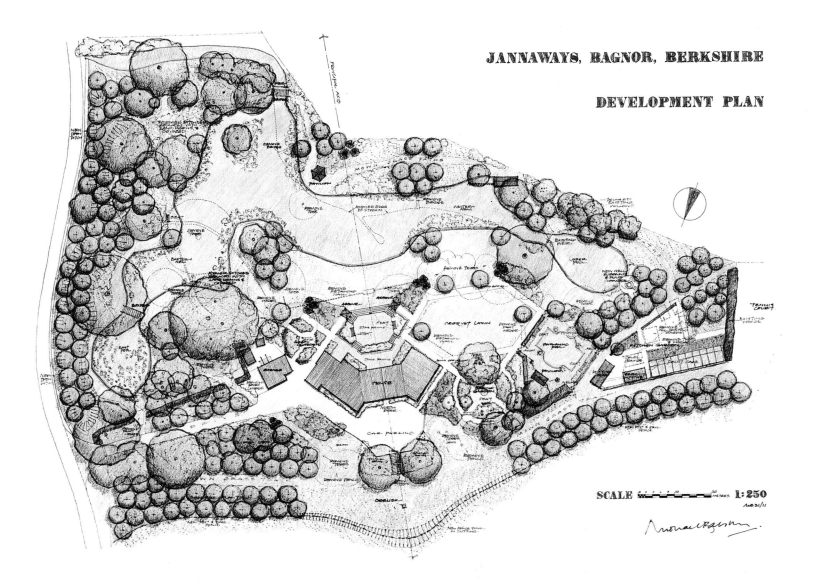

JANNAWAYS, BAGNOR, BERKSHIRE

DEVELOPMENT PLAN

SCALE 1:250

RIGHT: *The pavilions are built to match the details of the house and serve to extend the living space.*
BELOW: *Sketch for garden pavilions.*

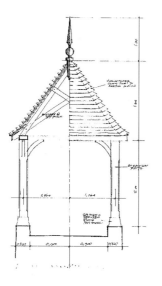

ABOVE: *View of the pavilions.*
LEFT: *Swimming pool with Lupinus hybrids in the foreground combine with fan palms in wooded planters to create a 'hot' planting scheme.*

ABOVE: *A long view over the lake giving the impression of a huge expanse of water.*

LEFT: *Water is as valuable for its reflections as for its movement. Here the lake becomes a mirror, reflecting autumn's colors.*

OPPOSITE PAGE: *House and pavilion as seen from the south boundary. The walk continues all the way around the lake.*

ROFFORD MANOR

ABOVE: *Gates to the courtyard were centered on the barn opposite and given new piers.*
OPPOSITE PAGE: *A small symmetrical ante-room was created around the door to welcome the visitor.*

Rofford Manor is perhaps the best known of my private gardens. My involvement came about in a curious way. Christopher Lloyd was being customarily irreverent about some of my more irrational (to him) thoughts about plants in one of his weekly articles for *Country Life*. Reading it, Hilary and Jeremy Mogford thought that I might be the person to help them. Thus began a long association that has spanned two private gardens and two hotel gardens.

Rofford Manor is a substantial traditional brick and tile house with outbuildings set on the flattish plain to the north west of the Chilterns. A kitchen garden and a herb garden were already in the making, and when I arrived on the scene borders were about to be started. The general proposals were entirely logical, and at this stage I merely tweaked what was already started and developed the planting plans. Even then I was attempting to introduce a slanting dynamic into otherwise symmetrical borders—a foretaste of Chelsea 1999 perhaps.

The next project was the swimming pool garden, where I tried to mitigate the baldness of the pool structure by planting close to the edges in raised stone planters. The billowing foliage breaks the hard line of the pool edge whilst modern cleaning gadgets are quite sufficient to pick up the odd leaf that drops in. Then came the green garden to the west side of the house in which the subtly different textures of yew and box and pleached limes in varying shades of green are a soothing contrast to the horticulture of the borders and rose garden.

The works have gone on over the years—improvements to the entrance court, the creation of a little gravel garden for the caretaker's cottage and a new greenhouse off the kitchen garden. They even rashly allowed me to interfere with the buildings, and I drew up a scheme for one of the barns as a banqueting hall. It was scarcely an economic use of an existing building but it made a wonderful place for a party. I advised, too, on the planting around the new lake in the low ground to the north west. With an extensive use of native species designed to encourage wildlife, we formed substantial new belts of trees that reshaped the spaces in a way that was more sympathetic to the natural lie of the land.

More recently we have extended the green garden to the west creating a large lawn retained by a long curving ha-ha to keep the cattle out. Overlooking and backing on to the rose garden is the new steep-roofed belvedere with views to the lake. This new work has drawn the entire garden together on the western side.

It has been a great satisfaction creating this garden with the Mogfords who work hard in the garden themselves. The creation has been truly a joint effort in which their contribution, in terms of ideas and sheer hard work, has complemented and reinforced mine. It is a model relationship that I believe has produced the best from all of us. If only it could happen more often.

RIGHT: *Pleached limes enclose the green garden.*

OPPOSITE PAGE, CLOCKWISE FROM LEFT: *Garden plan; aerial view of main entrance courtyard; main entrance and courtyard.*

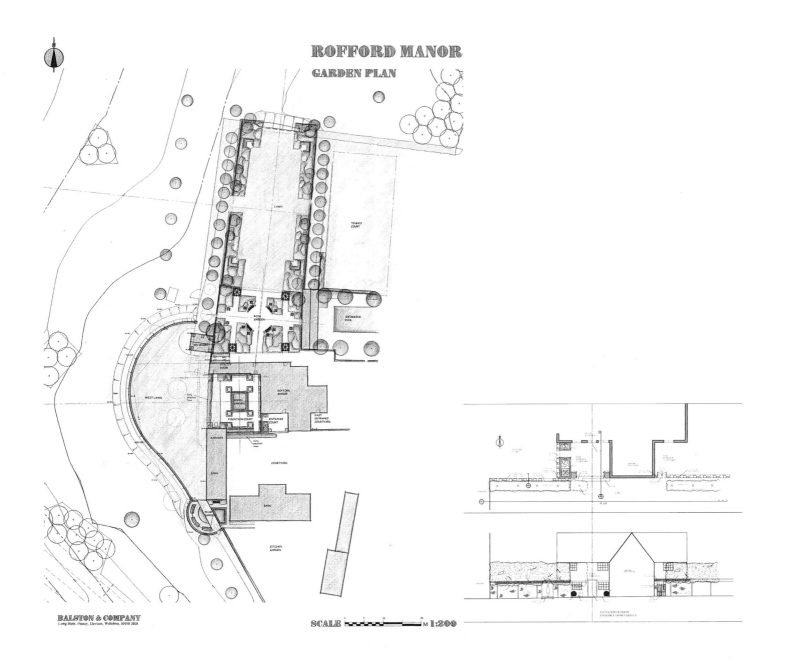

ROFFORD MANOR

GARDEN PLAN

BALSTON & COMPANY
Long Barn, Patney, Devizes, Wiltshire, SN10 3RB

SCALE M 1:200

ABOVE: *The path to the kitchen door through the green garden.*

LEFT: *Another area of clipped shrubs consisting of box and santolina in a rather more complex design on the east side of the house.*

OPPOSITE PAGE: *The restful green garden is dominated by clipped box and yew.*

RIGHT: *A view of the swimming pool through the pool house. The manipulation of light and shade is an essential part of the garden's design.*
BELOW: *Sketch of swimming pool and terrace.*

LEFT: *Clipped box in Versailles boxes are always useful in a garden at points of entry and exit.*

LEFT: *The rose garden that lies on the route to the swimming pool and the north-south axis of the garden. The obelisks are planted with clematis.*
OPPOSITE PAGE: *A casual way around the northeastern corner of the house where plants grow in the cracks in the paving.*

CUCKLINGTON HOUSE

Overlooking the Blackmoor Vale in Somerset, Cucklington House is perched on the side of a steep escarpment. It has sumptuous views to the west over a patchwork of farmland that still has its hedges and its cows. But as so often in England, good south-westerly views let in the south-westerly gales and when the weather is boisterous, raindrops travel upwards on the windows.

My involvement in this job, as ever, was by a somewhat circuitous route and I was taken on because of my enthusiasm for flooding a field to make a lake. My megalomaniac tendencies would have flooded the whole Vale if I had had half a chance. My client had vision and appreciated my ideas. Design sessions were long and hotly argued, fuelled by copious wine and sumptuous food. The process ensured that he fully identified with a design that truly belonged to him and the house. Although tiring, it was a thoroughly rewarding process.

As domestic jobs go, it was pretty big but absolutely my kind of area, combining buildings and landscape. It required much attention both at the planning stage and in the detailed drawings and specifications. We started with a careful survey to work out precisely the best views and vantage points. The layout of the new buildings and gardens was firmly based on this visual analysis. As well as the garden and its structure, the brief included a large octagonal conservatory at the same level as the house and an indoor swimming pool half buried into the hillside below. There were miles of retaining wall to build, paving to put down and beds to prepare. A tennis court was installed near the swimming pool and the great ha-ha constructed that separated the garden from the fields below. Construction was against an incredibly tight program, and we got off to a bad start with the site being under snow for an unreasonable length of time. But we achieved enough of the building works to have a major round of shrub and herbaceous planting in the winter of 1993 to 1994 prior to our deadline—a felicitous deadline if ever there was one...

The great party of July 1994 made all the blood, sweat, and tears worthwhile. Through the client's French connections, the food and wine were choice. There was a French theme and two or three hundred guests, I forget now, wandered round the garden dressed as revolutionaries or French chambermaids in their little black numbers. Cartloads of oysters from Brittany opened the eating, followed by terrines and pates, lobsters and quails, red meat and white and beautifully cooked vegetables.

But that, of course, was not the end. The lake, the raison d'etre of my appointment, was created. Then came the kitchen garden to supply a growing family as well as the next party. What a project—it was wonderfully extravagant and it built as strong a friendship as it did a garden. I can only count myself lucky to have been involved in such an exciting scheme.

FAR RIGHT: *Sketch for conservatory pineapple finial.*
RIGHT: *Sketch of alterations to front door.*
OPPOSITE PAGE, CLOCKWISE FROM TOP: *Garden plan; watercolor showing view from kitchen garden toward school house; watercolor of water feature and pool.*

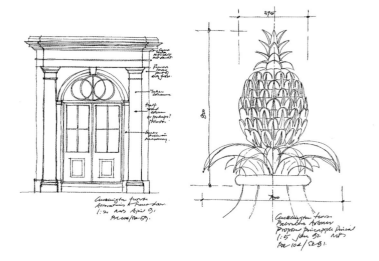

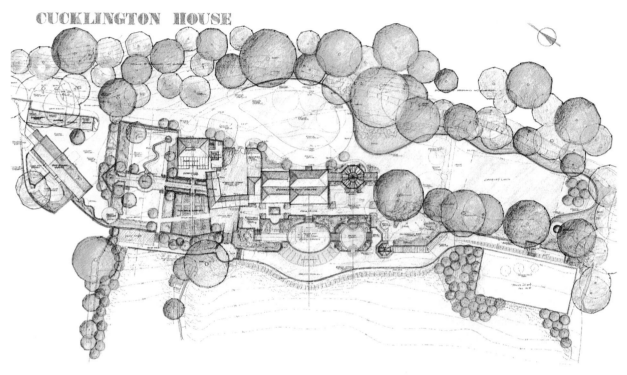

CUCKLINGTON HOUSE

GARDEN PLAN

SCALE 1:200

ABOVE: *An arbor in the kitchen garden beckons through the veranda terrace door.*

LEFT: *Textures were particularly exploited at Cucklington. This path is constructed in cobble stone.*

OPPOSITE PAGE: *A new door through an old wall leads to the veranda terrace.*

LEFT: *Granite setts contrast with bricks where a path leads up to the greenhouse and garages.*
OPPOSITE PAGE: *The kitchen garden lies to the north of the house. An arbor marks a junction of the paths.*

CLOCKWISE FROM TOP LEFT: *The glazed wall of the underground swimming pool with the belvedere prominent at the end; the view over the Blackmoor Vale from the belvedere is superb; at the northern end of the range of buildings is the old school house.*

OPPOSITE PAGE: *The house and some of its flanking buildings as seen from the lake below.*

HEATHER'S FARM

This job was the first that I carried out in conjunction with Joanna Wood, the interior designer, and Barrett Lloyd Davis, the architects. It was relatively ambitious in scope and based on a modest Sussex farmhouse and small-holding locked into large stretches of mature woodland. The landscape was agreeable and well-protected, but it had the disadvantage of being situated on the heaviest of mid-Sussex clays—positively a back-breaking site. However, the energetic Mr. and Mrs. Gregson were not in the least bit daunted and have turned it into a highly productive ground with ornamental and fruit trees racing away, a full kitchen garden and a big curved border that now looks almost mature. Again, I have been extraordinarily lucky with my clients, for they take advice and work hard to achieve the best possible result. Working in close collaboration with Joanna Wood and the architect we became a close knit team and the success of the overall scheme has owed as much to my clients input as it has to my own. A joint effort is so much more rewarding than lonely furrow ploughing.

Starting in late 1993 I found that works to the house were already under way, but that nobody had had much clue as to how the garden could or should be integrated. The drive and its flanking hedge followed an unfortunate route that divided the area around the house from the fields to the south. The key design gambit was to relocate the drive and break through the hedge into the field beyond. We then made a large circular lawn and enclosing it with a ha-ha, created the illusion of unimpeded space rolling away to the distant woods. This lawn formed the central feature around which the whole design revolved. It gave us the opportunity to create a long, curved, mixed border on the west side, `a la Anglesey Abbey, near Cambridge. I find this one of the most satisfactory ways of displaying a mixed bed as the relationship among groups of plants is constantly on the move as you walk around. From the mid-point of the border a route was made that led north through the newly created kitchen garden to a large greenhouse. West of this, against the boundary trees, we created a large, square sleeper-edged pond with a green oak pavilion on its axis. To the east of the circular lawn we terraced the rising ground into walks of cobnuts and walnuts that screened the farm buildings. Against the house we made a long stone terrace framing beds in which roses, *clematis*, jasmine, *eschscholzia* and *Solanum* luxuriate, along with myrtle, cistus and hebe.

The planting of the border was an interesting exercise. We backed it with a yew hedge planted with 60cm (2-feet) high plants, and now growing at 30cm (1-foot) a year. Behind we planted an orchard of apples, damsons and cherries, together with some ornamental trees. Structural plants in the border itself included *Amelanchier*, lilac, purple hazel, golden *Philadelphus*, *Forsythia suspensa* and many others. These were not chosen for their horticultural rarity–more for their good performance in the given conditions and their combination with the other plants. About sixty percent of the area was planted with summer herbaceous plants including such stars as *Crambe cordifolia*, irises and *Acanthus spinosus*, then *Macleaya cordata*, *Phlox paniculata* and *Eupatorium purpurea* that kept the flowering going well into the autumn. For the spring we inter planted with *Scilla*, *Chionodoxa*, *anenome*, and *crocus* with *Narcissus* behind in the orchard area. Then to hold it all together we spaced at regular intervals big clumps of *delphiniums* for the summer, *Cortaderia selloana* for the autumn and at a more closely spaced rhythm, *yucca* in the front. On the other side of the path, taking up the change in level to the circular lawn was a bank clad in box with *Crataegus oxycantha coccinea plena* planted at regular intervals. The border is conceived as a unit and highly structured but it has sufficient flexibility for the Gregsons to take it over and introduce their own plants in due course.

FAR RIGHT, RIGHT: *The curved border from the central arbor. The circular lawn lies to the left. The changing level of the border against the circular lawn is taken up by a box planted bank with standard thorns growing through.*
OPPOSITE PAGE, TOP: *Garden plan.*
OPPOSITE PAGE, BOTTOM: *Sketch of view across swimming pool.*

HEATHER'S FARM

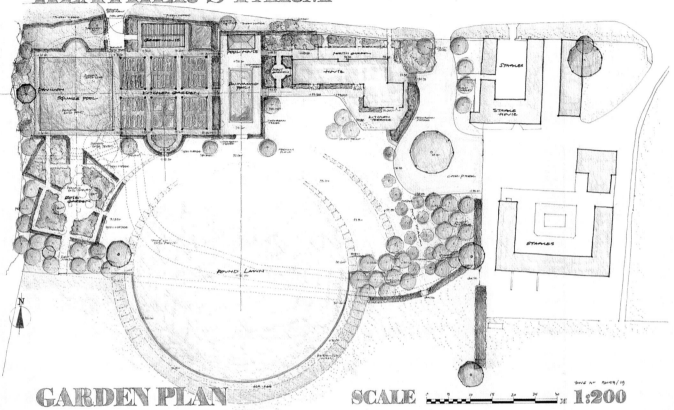

GARDEN PLAN

SCALE 1:200

ABOVE: *View through the kitchen garden to the pond arbor.*

RIGHT: *The pond arbor from the circular border.*

LEFT: *The pavilion overlooking the square pond.*

LEFT: *The circular border.*
OPPOSITE PAGE: *Door leading to the road from the north garden.*
FOLLOWING PAGES: *The circular lawn and park beyond from the kitchen garden.*

LOWER LYE

ABOVE: *The approach from the realigned drive illustrates that the way one gets to the house is fundamental to our perception and enjoyment of the house.*
OPPOSITE PAGE: *The rose garden stepping up the east side of the older part of the house.*

I have been lucky with some of the sites I have worked. Lower Lye is on the Wiltshire/Dorset border in the most sumptuous country. Lying in a ripple of ground on a southwesterly slope, the house has wonderful views towards Alfred's Tower above Stourhead to the west and over the Stour Valley. It is an inspiring site and my clients, Andrew and Belinda Scott, made the bold decision to rebuild part of the house and retain the site, rather than move elsewhere to accommodate their growing family more commodiously.

I was also fortunate in that I was appointed before they had re-planned the house, so that I could influence the siting and massing of its extension and of the outbuildings. The relationship of building to site is as much a landscape issue as an architectural one. How you approach a building, where the front door is, the space outside that welcomes the visitor, even the space inside the front door are all relevant to the journey through the landscape that terminates in the building. If these decisions are made irreversible before the landscape designer is consulted, then that journey can sometimes go badly wrong.

Nicky Johnson and Peter Cave were appointed architects and in a fruitful collaboration we planned a considerable complex of buildings and landscape that included the house, garages, a greenhouse and a swimming pool, as well as a croquet lawn and a grass tennis court and a rose garden. A building spine evolved along the contours with a garage court to the north and interlocking garden spaces opening out to the landscape. There was a strong sense of place and full advantage taken of the views.

Landscape works started in 1995, well in advance of the house, with the round lawn, sited at the end of the rose garden and looking out over a steep valley. Then we moved on to the drive. The old drive was direct and oblivious of the wonderful views that could be had from the higher ground. A re-routing of the drive could make the approach to the house really exciting. It was an expensive option but bravely agreed by Andrew and Belinda and inevitably it changed everyone's perception of the site. That complete, we immediately went into major earth-moving to get the site into shape before the works to the main building began. This afforded us the bonus of established grass areas before the house was re-occupied.

The planting, at least in the park, also had the advantage of an early start. We concentrated on natives like oak, lime and field maple, and supplemented them with more exotic species such as Black Walnut, Sweet gum, Tulip tree and Red Oak. The planting round the house, however, had to be delayed. Thus the rose garden, the big herbaceous border, the oval lawn and the walk down towards the round fountain had to wait until spring 1997. But growth has been good, and the garden is now looking reasonably mature with some of the more vigorous herbaceous plants ready for thinning. It will not be long before the garden will look as though it has been there forever, with its former layout a distant memory.

ABOVE: *The new wing of the house as seen from across the planting of hastas flanking the croquet lawn.*
OPPOSITE PAGE: *Garden plan.*

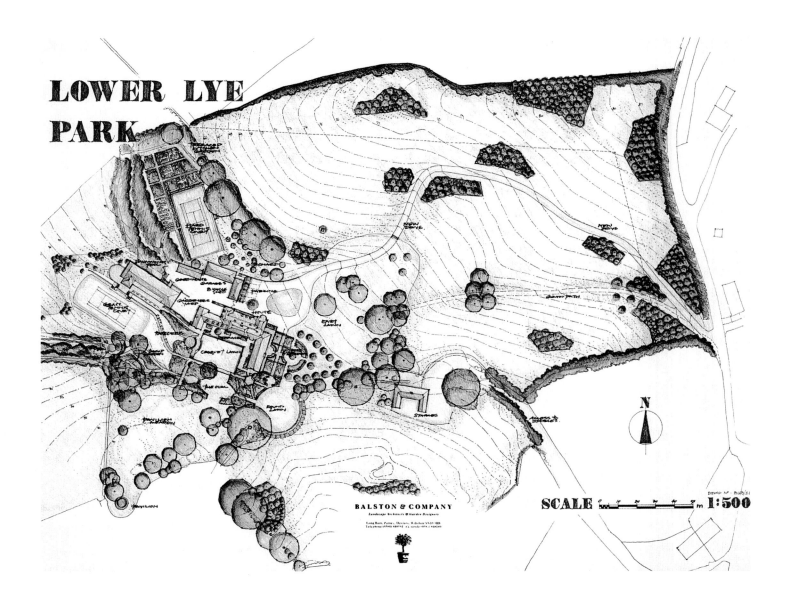

LOWER LYE
PARK

BALSTON & COMPANY

Landscape Architects & Garden Designers

SCALE   m **1:500**

LEFT: *The terrace adjacent to the old wing of the house.*
OPPOSITE PAGE: *The junction of the new and old wings as seen past the magnificent tulip tree that remained from the original garden.*

ABOVE: *A view through an existing beech hedge to a relocated urn.*
RIGHT: *A sundial at the junction of the new borders.*

ABOVE: *The herbaceous borders with the tulip tree beyond.*

LEFT: *The new herbaceous borders to the south of the swimming pool link. Their shape reflects the difficult modeling of the land.*

BELOW: *Sketch of croquet lawn and terrace.*

FOLLOWING PAGES: *The arbor encloses a very private space that will be hard to find once the climbers have grown up; the scented rose garden as viewed from the drawing room window.*

A LONDON GARDEN

This was an intriguing project that required an integration of the skills and imagination of the interior designer Joanna Wood, the architects Barrett Lloyd Davis, and myself. We had worked together before, but this was quite a formidable test of our ingenuity. There was not the scope for an extensive garden, but what we designed would have a particular impact on the interior, especially at basement level. We were fortunate in that the clients were young, and adventurous and between us we created an external space that comes as a wonderful surprise. It had been unpromisingly dark and unattractive; a pit that was surrounded on three sides by two-story buildings and on the west side by five stories. Now it is full of light and color, and gives the illusion of being far larger than its actual 27 square meters.

The size and shape of the space imposed great limitations on us, but also presented a terrific design challenge. One side was permanently in shade, and even where the sunlight did penetrate, it didn't stay for long. But the courtyard was of critical importance to the interior design of the lower floors, and we wanted to make the most of it. We gave the impression of a more generous space than was actually available by dividing the courtyard into three sections. This meant that the aspect from the conservatory that is attached to the kitchen was through trellis arches down to the covered seat on the garage wall. We used the finest natural materials outside, including sawn stone and planed and painted timbers, to complement the interior design. The garden furniture, seats, pots and lead water trough were all designed with the greatest care. And, of course, we also took pains to provide a rich growing medium in the beds so that the shrubs and climbers quickly and vigorously established themselves to extravagantly lush effect, especially on the trellis work. Despite the network of drains and services underground at this level, we were still able to create reasonably deep beds to support large shrubs such as *Acer palmatum*, *Skimmia foremanii*, *Pittosporum tenuifolium* and *viburnum x bodnantense*. And wreathing the trellis is white wisteria, trachelospemum, roses and clematis. As a final touch, we added dozens of handsome clay pots from the Landscape Ornament Company, which were filled with bays, box, marguerites, camellias and annuals.

We were unable to take full advantage of the possibilities presented by the terrace on the upper level because the required permissions to develop the roof space as a garden were unfortunately not available. Nonetheless it was a decent open area, which did not need to be blended with the interior, so we timber decked it, built fixed benches and put in planters and trellis work that now support shrubs such as *Fremontodendron californicum* and *Cytisus battandieri*, *Spartium junceum*, *Caryopteris x Clandonensis* and Rosemary, Lavender and Sage, and climbers include clematis, solanum, roses, honeysuckle, and hops.

ABOVE: *The use of trellis arches to create a succession of distinct areas giving the impression of more space. High quality furnishings are of the greatest importance in such a small area.* RIGHT: *Garden plan.*

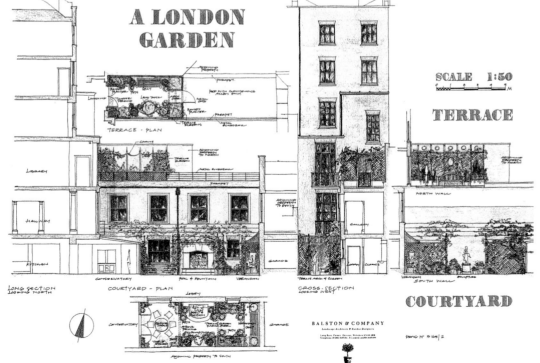

ABOVE: *Despite its unpromising situation, rich planting was achieved.*
TOP LEFT: *The lead tank and spout were custom made for the garden.*
LEFT: *Sketch for water feature and trellis.*
BELOW: *Sketch for water feature spout.*

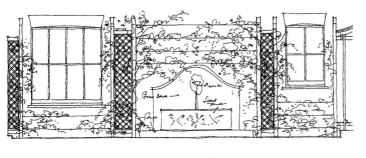

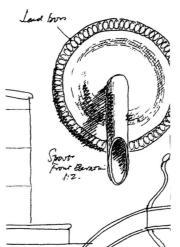

THE GRANGE

One good garden design relationship can often give birth to another. My long involvement with Rofford Manor brought forth just such a commission. Following a visit to Rofford in 1994, Bill and Linda Caldwell were sufficiently inspired to entrust me with a fundamental redesign of their garden at The Grange, a village house in West Sussex.

The Grange occupies a pleasant southerly slope stretching from the village street to the River Rother and is about 1.15 hectares (2.84 acres) in size. The house is constructed in stone, rendered on the garden side, with brick dressings and a tiled roof. It is largely Georgian and has an engaging asymmetry. It has stone boundary walls, and its lawns running down to the river are dotted about with interesting trees and shrubs dating from the time of the previous owner, a keen plant collector. There is a wonderful low-lying valley landscape across the river. My brief was to capitalize on the existing garden, but to create more places—areas to sit, to enjoy different times of the day, different activities, views and plant combinations. My clients wanted to enjoy some of the variety that they had seen at Rofford.

The possibilities were endless but as in most designs it was necessary to exercise a partial process of elimination based on financial constraints. Other important considerations were future labor requirements and costs involved in the garden's upkeep. There is no point in creating an elaborate garden, however beautiful, if it cannot be maintained. The general thrust of the design was suggested by the assets already on site—the character of the house, the views, existing free-standing walls and retaining walls, and the excellent plants already in

ABOVE: *The restful green carpet in the foreground becomes a vivid magenta once a year as the thyme flowers, changing the entire feel of this space.* OPPOSITE PAGE: *A formal parterre leads to the front door of this elegant village house.*

239

place. These factors tended to determine spaces, functions, and routes and my role was mostly one of reorganization bringing the whole garden into play, creating new kinds of spaces, and reinforcing the existing planting. As usual, I carried out a thorough survey and analysis of what was there. I then worked on different areas in a fairly loose sort of way to find how to make the most of them and at the same time best fit a coherent scheme.

In some designs there are overriding reasons for wholesale change, but this was not really one of them and a process of adjustments achieved better results. We worked up an overall plan fairly rapidly, followed by construction and planting details for each area as and when required. New planting areas were contained in a flow of shrubs and herbaceous perennials flowering throughout the year. But there were different emphases at different points—such as old-fashioned roses, mostly pink, near the entrance or the raised thyme lawn, rich purple in flower, on the lower terrace to the east. Off the conservatory terrace we created an oval lawn within the curve of an existing stone retaining wall, broken by a flight of steps leading down to a new croquet lawn. We planted these areas predominantly with shrubs but finished the design against the open lawns with a massive herbaceous border.

With clients keen on their horticulture and partially acid soil there is a greater range of plants here than in most other gardens I have undertaken. The flowering season is greatly improved and there are more durable textures. Spatially it seems a new garden and yet it holds on to all the principal elements that existed before. Over four years The Grange has achieved a new excitement of plant and place.

RIGHT: *Seats are so important in design—not only for a rest in the sun—but also as a focus of a layout.*
BELOW: *Preliminary study east of house.*
OPPOSITE PAGE: *Garden plan.*

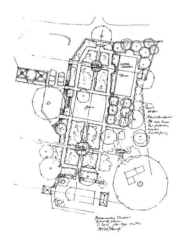

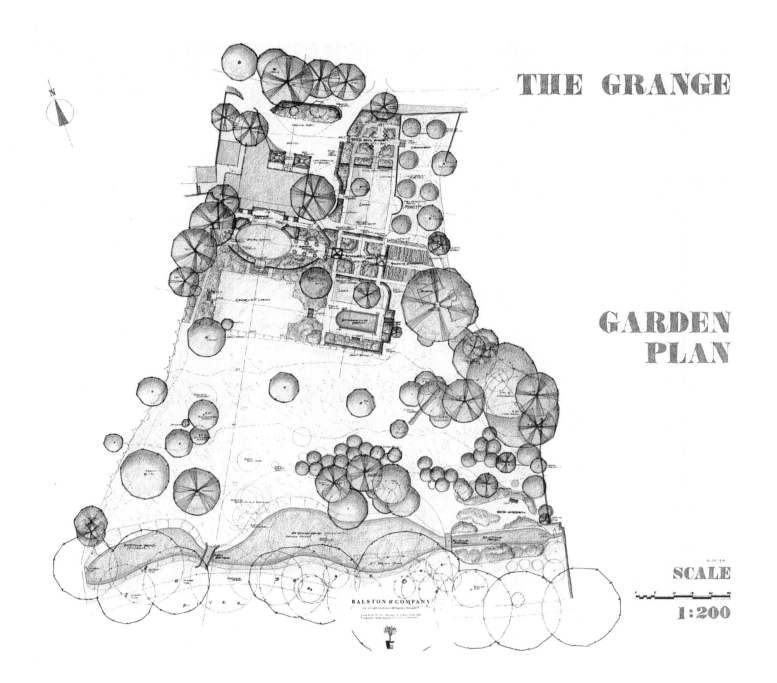

THE GRANGE

GARDEN
PLAN

SCALE

1:200

LEFT: *Urns are a useful contrast to plantings. Here in the planting bed, it defines an edge.*
OPPOSITE PAGE: *The long step flanks an oval lawn and leads down from the conservatory terrace.*

ABOVE: *Light and shade lead eye and foot from space to space.*
RIGHT: *The swimming pool was inherited from a previous scheme and planted around with shrubs to give privacy.*

ABOVE: *Plants that seem almost stemless like* Verbena bonariensis *are frequently used to give a light froth over a border.*

LEFT: *A view across the garden showing some of the mature trees and shrubs already on site.*

LEFT: *Perhaps the most telling feature of a good garden design is the manipulation of textures—so much more rewarding than the ephemeral of flowers.*

OPPOSITE PAGE: *Boxwood balls are useful for creating edges. In this case, they help define a path.*

FOLLOWING PAGES: *The pink-flecked lollipops of Rosa Heritage grown as standards create a unifying element on the axes of the rose garden.*

DAILY TELEGRAPH GARDEN

I have always been interested in show gardens, ever since I first exhibited at Chelsea in 1979. There is an enormous challenge in producing a convincing garden under show conditions, with limited build-up times and under intense professional and public scrutiny. For a variety of reasons I had not exhibited at Chelsea since 1986. During the interval the show had changed pretty dramatically. In particular, with corporate sponsorship, budgets had were significantly bigger and Chelsea had become a media event. However, I really only wanted to exhibit at Chelsea if I could design something that was forward-looking, using modern materials and not overburdened by tradition. Also, I wanted to be sure that the garden would be re-used after the show. It took some time to find the right sponsor, but eventually the Editor Charles Moore asked me to create a modern garden for the 1999 Show on behalf of *The Daily Telegraph*.

I had long been interested in tensile structures and admired the work of Frei Otto and Buro Happold and the way so many good modern architects use them in buildings. I felt that, at a small scale, they had an obvious application in gardens. For a show garden such structures could be used more in a dynamic, sculptural way than in a purely functional way. I thus developed a plan in which light canopies created a tension and movement that was picked up both in the structural elements, such as steps and decking, and in the diagonal lay of the planting. Although it was a minute garden, it was one of the most exciting that I had ever worked on. And it greatly helped to have an enlightened sponsor backing me all the way, as well as having the able technical expertise of Buro Happold to make the structures stand up.

The diagonal movement overlay a longitudinal organization. On one side was a decking walkway to make people feel as though they were actually inside the garden as they

ABOVE: *The canopies reach across the garden focusing attention on the rich planting border.*
OPPOSITE PAGE: *Lucien Simon's sculpture, 'Vein II' contrasts with the plantings and becomes a forward framing element.*

passed under the canopies. Next was a canal in three descending sections with a stepped lawn alongside opening out to the front and focusing on the elliptical stainless steel sanctuary at the rear with its flared trumpet-like canopy. Next to the lawn was a mixed border in which strong textural clumps picked up the booms of the canopies opposite. The design was an exercise in dynamic counterpoint, contained within a powerful, but light, framework in which deliberate contrasts between line and mass, texture and color, were exploited to create layers of interpenetrating spaces.

While the design was developing, I was approached by the curator of the RHS garden at Wisley, Jim Gardiner, to submit a garden for the Wisley Show Gardens area, and arrange for its sponsorship. Quite unexpectedly, here was the second use I was looking for. Thanks to further funding from *The Daily Telegraph*, the garden is now installed on a new site and looking better than ever. The advantage of the Wisley site is that it is on a significant slope so that you approach the garden from below coming up under the canopies. The vertical dimension seems to be more powerful.

For Chelsea, apart from the textural anchors, I concentrated on plants that could be in flower in the penultimate week in May such as *Cercis siliquastrum, Cornus kousa* and a variety of Rhododendrons like Souvenir de President Carnot, Daviesii, and Persil. We included climbing roses and used good sub-shrubs like Epimediums and Euphorbias. The taller herbaceous plants, like Irises, foxgloves and day lilies, emphasized the diagonal lay, while geraniums, Primula and Heuchera and masses of hostas and ferns ran under the shrubs. It was a deliberately rich melange pinned down by strong textural clumps of phormium, yucca and rosemary. It set off the spare framework of steel blue masts and white canopies to perfection.

For Wisley we thinned out the planting considerably and added plants to perform well at other times of the year. Some of the rhododendrons for instance disappeared to allow space for the remaining plants to grow. The garden is now in the capable hands of David Jewel and his staff and the planting is racing away giving it a precocious maturity. I have agreed with David that he should move plants in or take plants out as required. I firmly believe that the garden should not only be able to cope with change, but should actually welcome it. Gardening is a temporal art as well as a spatial one. Gardeners should be encouraged to experiment with plants. My role as a designer is to provide an inspiring structure within which these plants are used.

TOP: *Computer model.*
ABOVE: *The garden installed at Wisley.*

DAILY TELEGRAPH GARDEN — CHELSEA 1999

ABOVE: *The precision of the masts and booms on the viewer's side of the garden contrasts strongly with the billowing masses of vegetation.*

TOP LEFT: *The steps in the grass create a sense of space and distance in the small space of the garden. Plantings are chosen that flower at the end of May during the Chelsea Flower Show.*

LEFT: *Garden plan.*

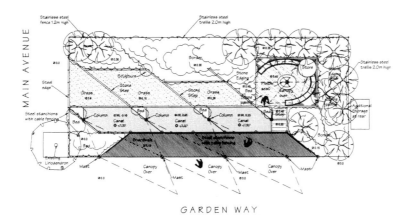

Dwg no B222/10A

BALSTON & COMPANY

Long Barn, Patney, Devizes, Wiltshire SN10 3RB

SCALE 0 1 2 3 4 5 ... 10   1:100

253

MARIO SCHJETNAN

TEZOZOMOC PARK

Azcapotzalco, Mexico City

ABOVE: *The lake at Tezozomoc evokes the ancient landscape of the Valley of Mexico.*
OPPOSITE PAGE: *The park provides recreational space for a crowded district of Mexico City.*

Tezozomoc Park is popular in several senses of the word. Located in a densely populated, working-class district of Mexico City, it is heavily used, especially on weekends, by people with little other access to public space. Commissioned by the borough of Azcapotzalco and built on a limited budget, it was also designed in a popular idiom, drawing on a familiar language of park design with particular reference to the history of central Mexico.

At the heart of the 30 hectare (75 acre) park, completed in 1982, is a lagoon that recreates the contours of the extensive system of lakes that once filled the Valley of Mexico; it is surrounded by low hills echoing the topography of the region. The historic lakes are long gone, filled by the relentless forces of urbanization; the mountains too are built upon. The park provides a physical trace or reminder of the landscape of the central valley in the years before the conquest. The effect is surprisingly familiar to those steeped in the English park tradition: the irregularly-shaped lake and undulating hills are evocative of the picturesque. Yet Tezozomoc is distinctly contemporary in its execution. It is built on a reclaimed industrial site; the mounds were made of earth from subway excavations; and recycled water—treated sewage from a nearby housing project—is used in the lake and for irrigation. The park itself was extensively reforested and there is a municipal nursery on the site which produces plants for use in the locality.

ABOVE: *One of sixteen obelisks depicting the history and myths of pre-hispanic settlements in the Valley of Mexico, now Mexico City.*

At the appropriate places along the edge of the lake are small plazas with obelisks indicating the location of the pre-Hispanic settlements that once ringed the valley of Mexico. With the collaboration of a biologist, a poet, and a historian, texts were chosen for these markers that illuminate the history, mythology, and ecology of the region. A small island in the lake even features a replica of the famous bronze sculpture by Olaguivel that stands in front of the Supreme Court Building in the Zócalo in the center of Mexico City. The sculpture depicts an eagle with a snake in its mouth perched in a cactus, a reference to the Aztec legend that Tenochtitlán—now buried under the Zócalo—was founded on the site of such an apparition. The combination of water, vegetation, aquatic birds, and interpretive material provides a glimpse into the past for the residents of Azcapotzalco, many of whom are migrants from other parts of Mexico with little prior knowledge of the history of the central valley.

The park's interpretive functions are complemented by tennis and basketball courts, a bike path, a cafeteria, an open-air auditorium, and a gymnasium. Recreational facilities are kept mostly to the periphery of the park; the bike path is separated from pedestrian circulation by a change in elevation. The original park design was quite eclectic, combining some axial paths and allées with more serpentine forms. But as the plantings have matured, the landscape has become more unified under the canopy of an urban forest. Tezozomoc is testimony to what can be achieved in the public sector, even with a modest budget and recycled materials.

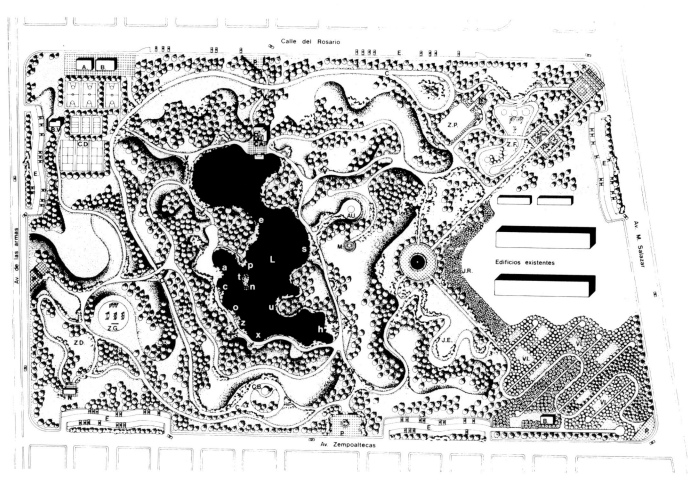

Calle del Rosario

Av. de las armas

Av. M. Salazar

Edificios existentes

Av. Zempoaltecas

CLAVES

P.	Plaza de acceso	EM.	Embarcadero	J.E.	Jardín de las esculturas
E.	Estacionamiento	AU.	Auditorio al aire libre	VI.	Vivero
A.	Administración	M.	Mirador	C.B.	Caseta de bicicletas
B.	Bodega	N.	Nucleo de servicios	C.	Ciclopista
C.D.	Canchas deportivas	Z.P.	Zona de patinaje	Z.D.	Zona de días de campo
B.V.	Baños y vestidores	Z.F.	Zona de juegos infantiles	Z.G.	Zona de gimnasia
CA.	Cafeteria	J.R.	Jardín de rosas	L.	Lago

Ruta Histórica

V.	Val e de México	O.	Coyoacan
e.	Ecatepec	z.	Tizapan
t.	Tlatelolco	u.	Culhuacan
a.	Azcapotzalco	x.	Xochimilco
p.	Tepeyac	s.	Texcoco
n.	Tenochtitlán	h.	Chalco
c.	Chapultepec		

TOP LEFT AND OPPOSITE PAGE:
*Formal in some areas, Tezozomoc is
more picturesque in others*
LEFT: *The park is enormously popular,
especially on weekends.*
BELOW: *Pedestrian and bike paths are
separated by a change in elevation.*

MALINALCO HOUSE

Malinalco, State of Mexico

Built in 1985 as a weekend house for his family, Schjetnan's Casa Malinalco is one of his first and still one of his most convincing mediations between architecture, topography, climate, and cultural history. Malinalco is a village of small houses and narrow streets in a subtropical valley 110 kilometers southwest of Mexico City. Still largely agricultural, it is divided into eight barrios each with a small colonial church dating from the 16th or 17th centuries.

The L-shaped house was built on the gently-sloping, 1,100-square-meter site of an old orchard. Living room, dining room, and kitchen are aligned along one axis, bedrooms along the other, creating something akin to a traditional cloistered courtyard. Taking advantage of the moderate climate and establishing strong links with the landscape, the common rooms are designed as a covered terrace entirely open to the courtyard on one side. On the other, shuttered windows overlook a second garden. Each bedroom also has its own private patio in the back; still more outdoor space is available on the flat roof.

ABOVE AND OPPOSITE PAGE: *Water crosses a cobbled courtyard and collects in a small pool.*

261

ABOVE: *In the south garden of the house are the remains of an old orchard.*

Heavily planted along its perimeters, the courtyard is paved at its center with long narrow cobblestones that create a geometric pattern. This patio is crossed by a small rill connecting a stone basin with a square reflecting pool adjacent to the living room. A bold pink wall faces one side of the garden; the color was selected by Luis Barragan, who felt it was necessary to set off the muted colors of the landscape. Below the house are the overgrown but still productive remnants of the orchard, including coffee, banana, mango, and citrus trees. Farther down the slope are surviving agricultural buildings, including a horse barn.

In a climate that includes rainy and dry seasons, the landscape is designed to minimize both runoff and irrigation. Cobbled pavers allow percolation of storm water; runoff passes through the orchard to an absorption well near the barn. Grey water from the house is recycled into the orchard through a sand filter.

With its simple lines, spare detailing, and Barragan colors, but with a plan suggestive of Spanish or Moorish cloister gardens, Schjetnan's Casa Malinalco is an eloquent combination of modern and traditional design, at once urbane and respectful of its village setting.

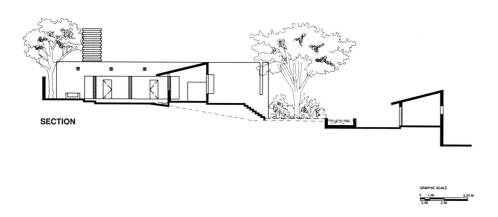

SECTION

GRAPHIC SCALE

0   1.00   5.00 M

0.50   2.50

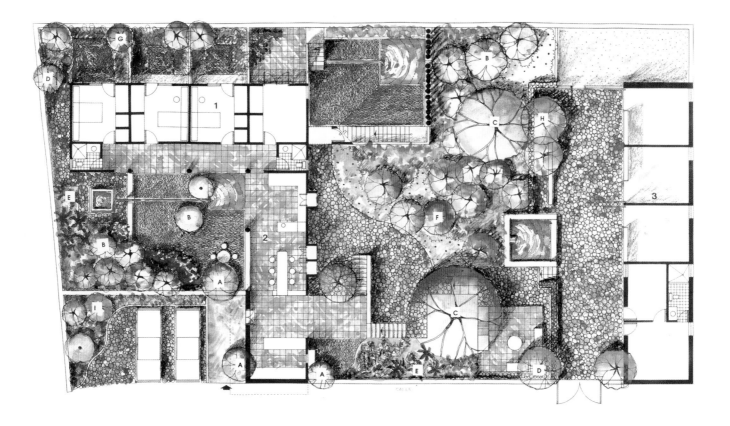

ABOVE AND OPPOSITE PAGE: *Views of the pool in the paved courtyard.*
RIGHT: *The orchard is irrigated with grey water from the house and rainwater captured in the pool.*

RIGHT: *One wall of the house was painted pink at the suggestion of architect and friend Luis Barragan.*
OPPOSITE PAGE: *The open-air living room is adjacent to the pool.*

ABOVE LEFT: *The L-shaped house frames two sides of a courtyard.*
LEFT: *The dining area and kitchen.*
BELOW: *The dining area, looking toward the living room.*
OPPOSITE PAGE: *View of preexisting orchard from the dining room.*

Mexican Cultural Center

Toluca, State of Mexico

Like his own house in Malinalco, the Mexican Cultural Center gave Schjetnan the opportunity to develop the connections between architecture, topography, and history, but this time on an large scale and in a public context. Completed in 1987, the Cultural Center was developed by the government of the state of Mexico on the 180 hectare site of a former hacienda west of Toluca, the state capital. The project encompasses a Museum of Modern Art, a Museum of Popular Culture, a Museum of History and Archaeology, and the main State Library, all set within a state park. It is adjacent to two universities, one public and one private, thus forming part of the capital city's most significant educational and cultural district.

Grupo de Diseño Urbano was responsible for the master plan for the entire park, for the landscape around the museums, and for the design of two buildings: the museums of modern art and popular culture. The museum campus is unified around a large concrete and stone plaza. A sequence of stepped platforms that stretch out over 250 meters, the plaza is on a north-south axis with a view toward the snow-capped peak of Nevado de Toluca. The plaza features a composition of standing volcanic stones in a large fountain, which gives the space the character of a ceremonial center. The hacienda's existing granaries and barns were adapted to become the popular culture museum, housing a large collection of crafts. The museum is organized around a central courtyard that features another large fountain; many of the museum's buildings also incorporate patios.

ABOVE: *Lobby of the Museum of Modern Art.*
RIGHT: *Isometric drawing of the Museum of Modern Art.*

The design of the Museum of Modern Art—a collaboration with Gonzalo Gomez Palacio Architects—was perhaps the most challenging aspect of this project. An unfinished, cone-shaped planetarium had to be incorporated into the plans. The planetarium was redesigned as an auditorium; exhibition spaces were placed around it; and a lobby, coffee shop, and bookstore were incorporated into the rest of the existing structure. The auditorium's exterior was surrounded by a set of concentric louvers that spread up and outward from the building; they sift natural light falling into the ring of galleries while seeming to levitate the cone. In order to reduce the visual impact of the whole structure and to link it with the truncated conical shapes of the volcanic landscape, the museum was partially concealed inside a berm which is in turn encased in a stone wall. Three elliptical excavations in the berm let additional natural light into the exhibition spaces. Schjetnan would later repeat this basic formula of a bermed, concentric construction at the Archaeological Museum of the Northern Cultures of Mexico, but with greater success: There, he would be unconstrained by an existing structure.

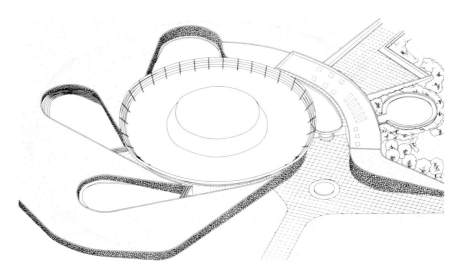

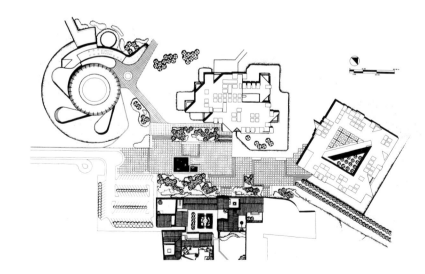

ABOVE: *The master plan for the entire park.*
LEFT: *The cultural center complex, with the Museum of Modern Art at the left.*

BELOW: *The plaza fountain.*
OPPOSITE PAGE: *The Museum of
Modern Art is partially buried by a
berm and ringed by a stone wall.*

Culhuacan Historical Park

Iztapalapa, Mexico City

ocated in southeast Mexico City, Culhuacan Historical Park is adjacent to a 400 year-old former monastery, San Juan Evangelista, perhaps the best preserved 16th century monastic structure in Mexico City. The building is now the Culhuacan Community Center and houses exhibitions of local history and architecture. It is part of the National Institute of Anthropology and History, which sponsored the restoration of the landscape, completed in 1988.

The site was once on the edge of a lake, and the remains of a pre-Hispanic embarcadero built upon by Spaniards are still visible adjacent to the monastery. The design used these ancient walls to frame a pool evocative of the vanished lake. Fragments of a colonial-era stone aqueduct were reused to provide water for the pool. On a newly-constructed raised platform between the water and the exposed monastery walls is an area for cultural events, including a stone-lined performance space surrounded by steps. Along another side of the pond is an area for passive recreation shaded by willows.

The simple palette of stone walls and pavers and the use of basic geometric forms creates material and formal continuities with the existing building. The different levels separate different programs, but they also evoke the archeological character of site. At about one hectare (2.5 acres), Culhuacan Historical Park is one of Schjetnan's smaller projects. But his attention to the topography and history of this site was important in the development of later, more ambitious works such as the Archaeological Museum of the Northern Cultures of Mexico in Chihuahua.

ABOVE: *This rendering by Brian L. Rothman suggests the site's appearance prior to the Conquest.*
OPPOSITE PAGE: *The reinterpretation of the original spring and water spout.*

Malinalco Golf Club

State of Mexico

Schjetnan's work at the Malinalco Golf Club ranged from broad-stroke planning to detailed design. His principal contribution is found in the Club's entry sequence, which includes a large square vehicular plaza behind massive stone walls, adjacent to shops and a pedestrian plaza that he also conceived. Schjetnan was additionally responsible for the design of streets and parking; he collaborated with master planners and golf course architects on the contours of the course itself and on the locations of lakes, cart paths, and service areas. He designed at the smaller scale of individual landscape features and recreation areas, orchestrating walls, waterfalls, and plantings, especially near the main club house and tennis courts.

Completed in 1993, Schjetnan's designs for the Malinalco Golf Club draw on several distinctive features of the regional landscape. The club lies in a lush agricultural valley surrounded by high cliffs, one of which boasts a pre-Columbian temple and fortress complex. The terraced landscape around Malinalco is divided by a network of dry stone walls that define individual property holdings. Consistent with this vernacular tradition, native stone was used extensively at the club for walls and street surfaces; indigenous trees and

ABOVE: *Dry stone walls (tecorrales) recall the surrounding agricultural landscape.*

other plants well-adapted to the subtropical highlands were planted along the roads. The detailing in the streetscaping is particularly effective: Small pavers make a solid surface for vehicles, while larger stones mark the medians and street edges. Trees are planted directly in the stone margins, shading the street. To the side, dense plantings of flowering shrubs provide a visual buffer between the street and golf course. A similarly fine level of detailing is found around the clubhouse and tennis courts. Stone walls divide gardens from children's play facilities; they also form small waiting areas near tennis courts. Grass steps and stone risers surround one of the courts, providing extensive if informal seating for those watching the matches.

Perhaps the most imposing feature of Schjetnan's work at the club, however, is the entry plaza. It is cut out of an imposing wall that steps downhill along the public road; purple metal gates lead to a 33 by 33 meter court with concentric pavers and a stone fountain at its center. Walls framing the entry plaza and fronting the street were constructed from massive boulders unearthed during golf course construction. At once ancient and modern in character, the plaza recalls the great scale of pre-Columbian construction even as it evokes the spare geometries of Luis Baragan's now largely lost compositions of volcanic stone, metal gates, and fountains at El Pedregal in Mexico City.

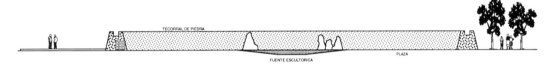

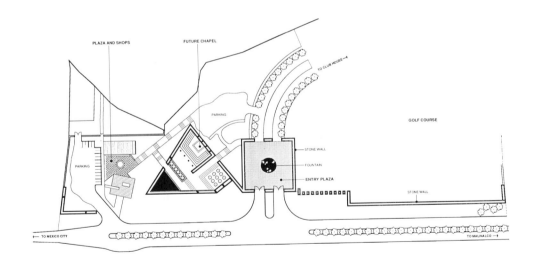

TOP LEFT: *View of lake, club house, and golf course.*
MIDDLE LEFT: *Section through entry court.*
LEFT: *Entry plan showing location of court, future chapel, and walls.*

ABOVE: *Detail of cascade.*
LEFT: *Entry median and stone walls leading into the golf club.*

LEFT: *Past the entry plaza, the views open up to the golf course and the valley.*
BELOW: *View of cascade and man-made lake.*

FOUNTAINS

Ofininas en el Parque, Monterrey, Nuevo Leon
Grupo Nacional Provincial, Coyoacán, Mexico City

ABOVE: *Oficinas in el Parque sculpture fountain with marble slabs by Maia Biblos and Mario Schjetnan.*
OPPOSITE PAGE: *Detail of the fountain.*

Work at Oficinas en el Parque corporate buildings in Monterrey, Nuevo Leon, was completed in 1999. Landscape elements include an entry plaza, gardens, and fountains, which knit together two slender office towers. The plaza is paved with irregularly-cut local stones and features a fountain of tilted marble slabs of various sizes; lights and jets are set into a concrete base. Surrounding plantings are composed primarily of cactus native to the region. The fountain's slabs are quarried from a stone similar to that which forms the mountains visible from the site; together, marble and cactus are intended to evoke the character of the region.

The main garden is organized around a reflecting pool that forms a podium for one of the towers. Taking advantage of the sloping site, GDU designed for this pool an imposing curved retaining wall that doubles as a cascading fountain. The garden is planted with oaks and framed on two sides by a yellow stucco wall.

BELOW: *Entry plaza with native plants in Oficinas en el Parque.*

The corporate complex for **Grupo Nacional Provincial,** completed in 1994, is located in the redesigned and reconstructed buildings of a university campus damaged in an earthquake. Grupo de Diseño Urbano was retained by Augusto Alvarez Architects to create a plan for the landscape spaces between the buildings, which are connected by porticoes.

The principal open space at the complex contains a water feature that is interesting both from design and engineering perspectives. The client required a cooling system for the computer equipment concentrated in one of the buildings. The original engineering scheme called for a visually intrusive tower some 36 feet high. Schjetnan's solution, which was constructed instead, consists of two basins with 112 water jets about six feet high and a capacity of 640 cubic meters. The jets cool the water, which is then piped inside to cool the air in the building.

While functioning as part of the air conditioning system, the fountains also mask urban noise and provide a pleasant outdoor gathering space for company employees. The space is nicely detailed: platforms, seating walls, and walkways reminiscent of Schjetnan's work at Culhuacán are made of Santo Tomás chipped marble and float above the water, which is surrounded with cobbles of pale river stone. Existing clusters of cedar trees were incorporated into the design and complemented with simple massed plantings of evergreen shrubs and roses.

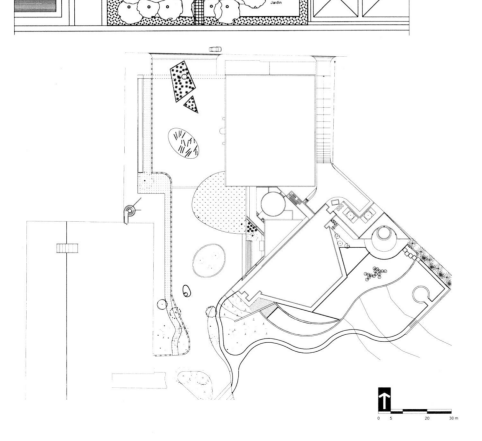

LEFT: *Plan of main courtyard fountain in Grupo Nacional Provencial.*
BELOW LEFT: *Plan of Oficinas en el Parque.*
BELOW: *View of courtyard fountain in Groupo Nacional Provincial from surrounding arcades.*

THIS PAGE AND OPPOSITE PAGE:
Views of fountain in Grupo Nacional Provencial which serves as the cooling system for buildings' air conditioning.

Archaeological Museum of the Northern Cultures of Mexico

Paquimé, Casas Grandes, Chihuahua

Paquimé, at Casas Grandes in Chihuahua, is the most significant archaeological site in northern Mexico. Built beginning around 700 AD and abandoned in the mid-14th century, the city was a center of the pre-Columbian culture that stretched from the desert regions of Chihuahua and Sonora into the southwestern United States. Located in a wide basin with expansive views toward the Sierra Madre, the site is noted for extensive remains including pyramids, ball courts, platforms, kivas, and multi-story, rammed-earth houses. It also has yielded numerous artifacts, especially pottery, jewelry, and carvings. At the instigation of the National Institute of Anthropology and History, Grupo de Diseño Urbano was retained to design a museum adjacent to the site. The building was intended to house the collection of artifacts, interpret site history, and explain strategies for research and preservation at the ruins.

Design was guided by the strong, simple geometries of the historic structures and by the extreme—yet extremely fragile—qualities of the desert environment. The result, completed in 1995, is as much landscape as architecture. Organized around a large circular courtyard open to the sky, the building is half buried in a berm planted with desert grasses

ABOVE: *A rectangular court that resembles a dry wash looks out toward distant mountains.*

and cactus. While diminishing the building's visual impact on the exposed site, the berm also provides the museum with some shelter from blazing sun and dust storms in summer, cold winds in winter. Exterior walls blend with the colors and textures of the desert: curved surfaces are faced in local, rust-brown volcanic stone; planar elements are made of buff-colored concrete.

Entry to the museum is gained by crossing a broad stone plaza and descending wide stairs. Inside, exhibition spaces surround the central patio, while three smaller courtyards of different shapes and themes introduce natural light into the galleries and create a transition between the building and the larger landscape. The first is a circular patio planted with Sonoran desert plants; the second a triangular court with pines evocative of the Chihuahuan sierra; and the third an elongated rectangle suggestive of an arroyo or dry wash that frames a view toward a distant mountain altar. Flat roofs on top of the exhibition space provide additional views over the archaeological site and its expansive surroundings; the roof is accessible from the central patio or the entry plaza.

Visually discreet, the building is a remarkably sensitive intervention in a culturally and environmentally delicate context. It suggests the extent to which contemporary architecture might further both topographical and historical interpretation.

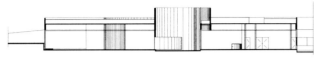

CORTE LONGITUDINAL 1.

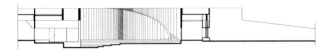

CORTE LONGITUDINAL 2.

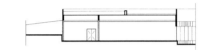

CORTE LONGITUDINAL 3.

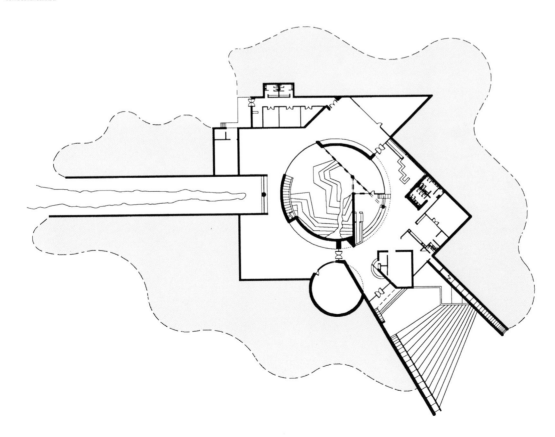

BELOW: *The museum's central patio is open to the sky.*
OPPOSITE PAGE: *A circular court evokes the landscape of the Sonoran desert.*

SPANISH TROPICAL GARDEN

Southern Florida

The renovation of this garden and residence involved several programmatic elements, including the addition of a new pool, pool house and recreation pavilion, and incorporation of a large spider-shaped sculpture.

"My first concern," says Jungles, "was to bring back the grandeur of the house and its historic walls so that all the elements of the project could relate to each other."

He designed a green plaza to replace the existing circular driveway and crowded foundation plantings at the front of the house. He then created a dramatic garden gateway that mirrors the scale and the stone of the Spanish colonial home's front entrance.

"I wanted a ceremonial entrance to the spectacular space at the back of the house where art, architecture, and garden design mix in a way that manages to be both contemporary and traditional."

ABOVE: *An intimate seating space was incorporated into a quiet area of the front garden. The Cycad in the middle ground is an* Encephalartos ferox *from Southern Africa.*
OPPOSITE PAGE: *An elevated plane of zoysia grass and saturnia stone replaced the existing circular driveway. Keystone from the previous driveway was reused for the parking court.*

RIGHT: *Two South American oil palms frame a view of the front door.*

The garden has an incredible palette of plant materials with contrasting and complementing textures and volumes. South American oil palms, tropical black bamboo, and an African Mahogany tree create an enormous scale that helps put the house and spider-like sculpture, emerging from a bed of—what else?—variegated spider plant, into proper perspective.

"The diversity and juxtaposition of materials in this garden help blend the noble architecture of the original house with the more modern design of the pool house and swimming pool," says Jungles.

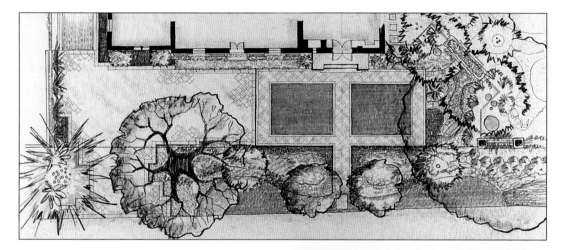

ABOVE: *Drawing of the original front garden concept. The proposed large canopy tree shown on the left was replaced by two South American oil palms to balance the large African mahogany tree on the right.*
LEFT: *Detail of stone walk.*

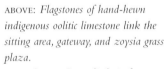

ABOVE: *Flagstones of hand-hewn indigenous oolitic limestone link the sitting area, gateway, and zoysia grass plaza.*

LEFT: *Orange Bromeliads in foreground are* Aechmea blanchettiana *'Orange Form' from Brazil.*

RIGHT: *The large-leaf plant climbing the royal palm is* Philodendron wilsoni. *Jungles brought this and many other plants, usually as cuttings, from Roberto Burle Marx's garden in Brazil.*

OPPOSITE PAGE: *Zoysia grass and saturnia stone plaza. The fuzzy palms on the left are* Coccothrinax crinita *from Cuba.*

ABOVE: *View toward the grotto garden from the loggia. The Bromeliad in the pot is* Neorgelia *spp. 'Bossa Nova'.*
RIGHT: *Original concept plan of the rear garden. The large, level lawn area serves as a green patio for entertaining.*
OPPOSITE PAGE: *(Left) View from the grotto garden toward the open lawn. The strong swath of color in the center is the rhizomaceous Begonia 'Black Velvet.'.*
(Right) View from the rear garden toward the front garden.

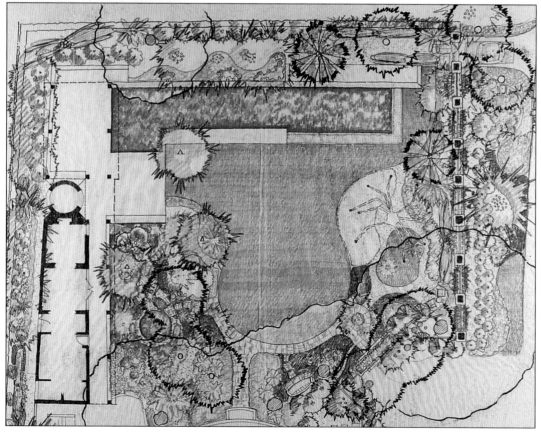

ABOVE: *The pool house/recreation pavilion was designed by architect William Bialosky in collaboration with artist Jackie Ferrara.*

LEFT: *View of the grotto pond and pool house/recreation pavilion.*

RIGHT: *Huge, majestic live oak trees provide the proper light and moisture for the understory plantings to flourish. Large boulders function as resting places.*

ABOVE: *View of the lap pool (designed by architect Bialosky in collaboration with artist Ferrara), the historic stone wall, and a sculpture by Louise Bourgeois. Variegated spider plant and river rock paths form the ground plane beneath the sculpture.*

LEFT: *The hand-hewn oolite stone path functions as a boarder for the lawn and as an access to the spa and to the gateway.*

SIMS GARDEN

Coral Gables, Florida

This garden is an excellent example of how the Jungles/Yates team can transform an unremarkable, suburban house and lot into livable art. The owners wanted a bold and playful anything-goes atmosphere. The overall project design evolved around Debra Yates' award-winning serpentine mural wall that runs along the back of the property, enlivening the garden from one end to the other.

"Having creative carte blanche and knowing that you would see only sections of the wall at any one time allowed me to visualize bold, crazy colors, and forms," says Yates, who was also inspired by Roberto Burle Marx. "Roberto was not afraid to use strong color or unusual geometric shapes in his gardens."

The compositional rhythm and color of the mural imparts a musical, be-bop feeling to the various spaces it inhabits. Tall colorful plantings of Tabebuia and bougainvillea behind the wall create privacy as well as the feeling that the garden backs up to the woods' edge.

The swimming pool's water jets add to the festive atmosphere. A variety of hardscape materials combined with a diverse collection of rare tropical palms, flowering trees, and indigenous plants give an overall sense of warmth and richness to the design.

The vibrant color scheme of the house and the redesigned outdoor areas help integrate the interior, the garden, and the exterior furnishings.

ABOVE: *(Left) A walkway of free-float-ing pre-cast keystone slabs creates a circuitous approach to the entrance. (Right) Palm trees enrich the front garden. The palm to the right is* Livistona rotundifolia, *from Malaya.* RIGHT: *The garden plan allows for many different spatial experiences within the compact site.*

LEFT: *Multi-trunk hurricane palms,* Dictyosperma album, *from the Mascarene Islands create vibrant shadows around the pool. The playful use of color enlivens the garden.*

ABOVE: *View from the lanai. A seat ledge in the pool encourages conversation.*

RIGHT: *The lanai serves as an extension of the interior living room. A privacy wall incorporates moss and epiphytic plants.*

OPPOSITE PAGE: *The Jungles-designed lanai, pool deck, and pool, blend into a generous, often-used space.*

FOLLOWING PAGES: *Views of the swimming pool.*

STEVEN STIMPSON

Cascade Pool

Central Massachusetts, 1999
Hart Associates, architects

Surrounded by an upland mixture of oak, maple, beech, hemlock and pine, Cascade Pool House is perched at the edge of a bluff sixty feet above a river. The entry drive approaches from the north and curves through native woodland alongside a crab apple orchard, the peaceful scene belying an interlocking drama of topography, hydrology and geology that awaits on the south side of the residence. Couched in the language of local agricultural traditions and architectural styles, the arrival sequence is a demure foil for the visual and material intensity at the heart of the site.

Emerging from the shaded forest into the open arrival court, visitors are met by a wide granite fieldstone wall that defines one side of the arrival area. This wall is a key compositional line that creates a subtle spatial volume and stitches the sloping grid of the orchard to the orientation of the house. The wall's detailing, from its unusual dimensions to the fact that it stands free from neighboring wall segments rather than returning as a continuous element, foreshadows the extensive stone infrastructure on the south side of the residence. A bed of laurel, rhododendron, vinca and European ginger accents the main entrance and softens the edge of the parking court where it meets the house foundation.

As one moves around to the south side of the residence, everything changes as the structurally complex interplay of water and topography becomes apparent. The landscape's

ABOVE: *A walkway below the cascade offers an intimate experience of falling water and sparkling mist. The right side of the walk is a reservoir that catches and recycles the water.*
OPPOSITE PAGE: *The pool's shape works with the existing forest frame and hillside contours to emphasize a sense of prospect. Sky and water reflect each other.*

orthogonal frames give way to a series of massive, arcing retaining walls. Each stone arc is a terrace that relates to adjacent rooms of the house — a kitchen garden, a dog run, a living/dining patio, a swimming pool off the exercise room. Together, the loosely concentric slices form a multi-level platform that holds the house into the hillside, and corresponds to rounded contours that descend to the river. The convexity of the terraces emphasizes that this is a place of prospect.

Set into the lowest of the three terraces, the pool interrupts the sweeping stone arc to release a waterfall. The pool challenges conventional form and is shaped to relate the house outward to the view (framed in part by the adjacent white pine). Meticulously crafted, the weir edge consists of an inner gunite wall and an outer concrete wall with a fieldstone veneer and a battered granite cap. The waterfall is perfectly placid as it flows over the cap. It then varies from a streaming sheet at high volume to a sparkling curtain at low volume that catches on the stone underneath. At any level, the sound of falling water permeates. Uplights magnify the liquid flow at night. From above, the pool — itself sometimes appearing as a sliver of atmosphere hovering in the treetops — reflects passing clouds and echoes distant wet meadows across the Concord River.

In some instances the degree of high tech manipulation at the Cascade Pool House is evident, such as the ability of the zero-edge pool overflow to be adjusted to cascade at three different volumes. In other cases, state-of-the-art engineering is cloaked in low tech craft, such as the simple bronze gate that appears to catch innocently in the stone threshold but whose operation is monitored by a concealed security system. Throughout, a consistent logic of materials reveals certain attitudes. For example, bluestone is intended to have a sense of geologic layering to it. Never used simply as a veneer, the four to six-inch thick pieces always appear in section, a quarried aesthetic that speaks of solidity and terrestrial structure. Overall, crisp delineations and the dynamic slicing of the terrace walls achieve a memorable transition from interior space to the exterior experience of the greater landscape.

ABOVE: *The stair from the upper terrace is oriented to intersect the pool edge and to move outward toward the greater landscape.*

RIGHT TOP: *A perspective sketch of the arrival court as the drive emerges from the shaded forest.*
RIGHT BOTTOM: *View through maple trees over the court wall and out to the young orchard.*
BELOW: *Site plan.*

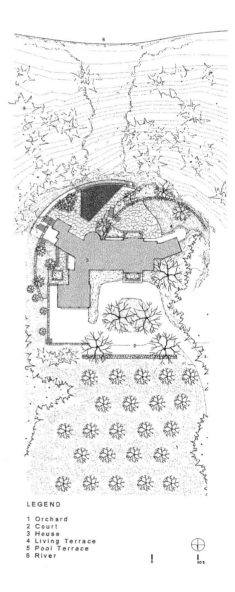

LEGEND

1 Orchard
2 Court
3 House
4 Living Terrace
5 Pool Terrace
6 River

Cascade Pool

ABOVE: *At the top of the cascade water glides over a granite cap. On the right end of the weir a snapping turtle sculpture guides current away from the wall.*

RIGHT: *Amelanchier foliage filters sight lines down to the pool. In the foreground, a ring of perennials outlines the edge of the upper living terrace.*

ABOVE LEFT: *The stone wall that defines one edge of the arrival court is composed of freestanding segments that slide past each other.*

LEFT: *Inside the arcing stone retaining wall granite steps negotiate small level changes.*

OPPOSITE PAGE: *Planted on a staggered grid, the orchard will mature into a strong spatial structure set against the native forest.*

FOLLOWING PAGES: *Individual terraces spill concentrically outward from the house. On the lowest level, the solidity of the encircling wall changes momentarily to shimmering liquid as the pool breaks through the stone arc.*

HAWK RISE

Nantucket, Massachusetts, 2001
Lyman S.A. Perry Architects, Inc., architects

ABOVE: *Throughout the designed landscape the use of stone is deliberately bold and minimal, bringing forth a dynamic dialog between macro and micro scales.*
OPPOSITE PAGE: *A layered landscape captures imagination and brings depth to the perception of site.*

Not invisible, but more sensed than seen, the interplay of glacial history and ocean expanse at Hawk Rise creates an impression of immensity within which resides an array of more detailed experiences. A shrub barren upland bracketed by beech stands, sassafras colonies and tupelo wetlands, the site's vegetation gives clues to soil conditions, hydrology and degree of exposure to the elements. Throughout the thirty-acre property a minimized palette of plant materials and simplified, pure forms reveal a designed landscape whose character is simultaneously rich and stark, vast and intimate, current and timeless.

Long hedgerows and stone walls organize the property into a collection of open pockets that hold the main house, guest house, garage, pool, pool house, tennis court and five future family residences. During construction, seventy-five native scrub oaks were transplanted to surround new elements with site-specific plantings. Several of the most gnarled oaks, stunted by salt air and strong winds, were pruned and replanted in the arrival area to highlight their natural distortions and mottled bark. The entry drive, designed to accentuate topography, enters from the south and traverses rolling dips and knolls and skirts contours before arriving at the main house, guest house and garage. Stone clad and hunkered into the earth (one steps down three feet to enter the house), these structures appear to catch and distill the undulating land into a singular plane that then descends toward the ocean from the north side. Architecture and landscape are knit together by a continuous band of stone that runs

ABOVE: *A long view down one of the arm-like walls that bracket the central lawn.*
OPPOSITE PAGE, LEFT: *Site plan.*
OPPOSITE PAGE, RIGHT: *Mowed paths meander through the wildflower meadow.*

the length of the south façade. Appearing alternately above ground as a freestanding wall, then slicing through earth to retain the grade around a sunken garden, then piercing the house itself to become an interior wall and chimney, this artful component represents significant collaboration between architect and landscape architect.

A second important result of the shared design process is the placement of the residence. Instead of locating the sizeable structure at the water's edge, a decision was made to pull the building back into the site, gaining elevation, valuable foreground and optimized sight lines. The journey through the site is enriched, as one first travels the shrub moorland by car, arrives at the house, and then moves through layers of terrace, lawn, wildflower meadow, scrub oaks and bluff by foot. Visible as a destination but not interrupting the visual connection between the main house and the ocean, a swimming pool, pool house and pergola sit down by the water's edge. In essence, the program has been attenuated to stretch the length of the site.

Emerging from grade, massive stone arms reach down the east and west sides of the wide north terrace and lawn. Part boundary, part visual aid to guide perceptual progress through the landscape, the stone walls align with existing scrub oaks and long views to the harbor. Rather than compete with the magnificent setting, the elevated north lawn and below it the wildflower meadow heighten awareness of the prospect. The resulting scale and simplicity of the space are striking. Native and planted vegetation push on the outside of the inner cultivated area, seasonal color and texture contrasting with the purity of the smooth grass surface. There is a crisp resonance to the ramped, architecturally banked expanse of lawn that speaks to the monumentality of the ocean without challenging it. It is a reminder that glaciers, the ocean and man all possess the ability — although working at notably different rates — to radically transform topography.

NANTUCKET HARBOR

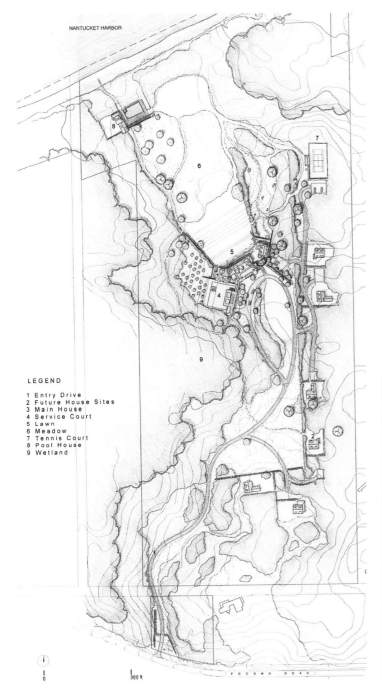

LEGEND

1 Entry Drive
2 Future House Sites
3 Main House
4 Service Court
5 Lawn
6 Meadow
7 Tennis Court
8 Pool House
9 Wetland

300 ft
0

THIS PAGE: *Detailed moments of purity and of contrast between the native and the designed landscape.*
OPPOSITE PAGE: *An unusual degree of collaboration between architect and landscape architect resulted in a symbiotic use of stone. Granite and bluestone move effortlessly between interior and exterior spaces.*

ABOVE LEFT: *A "water hedge" sprays up from the island. The pool is divided to provide a play area and lap lanes.*

LEFT: *The pool terrace is a final built edge atop the bluff before the terrain gives way to the ocean shoreline.*

OPPOSITE PAGE: *Pergola columns frame serene twilight at the pool.*

FOLLOWING PAGES: *Massive, stepped stone walls reach outward from the house, shaping the view and imbedding the inhabited landscape into the existing contours.*

COVE HOUSE

Coastal Massachusetts, 2001
Thompson and Rose, architects

Straightforward, refined elements and an emphasis on materiality qualify this young residential landscape as a future hallmark of SSA's design approach. Intersections, adjacencies, and edges are carefully considered and consistently treated in a manner that brings clarity and coherence to the site. From the outset, one has the sense that the site design conducts movement and perception, leading sequentially from the well-defined arrival court eventually to the open expanse at the ocean's edge. There is a visual energy manifest in the juxtaposition of terse, eloquent walls and purposeful plantings. Stone and wood surfaces are crafted to call out functional areas: broad slabs of lavender bluestone in the entry walk; crisp wood decking around the pool (secured with internal fasteners that avoid the need for nails and leave the surface unmarked); radial wood decking banded by stone on the west terrace. Hedge lines and tree groupings fortify spatial volumes, screen boundaries, frame views and pose as sculptural accents.

The most notable feature of this compact site are the low, primarily freestanding stone walls that arc around the oval play lawn elevated above the waterfront. The first wall stretches across the west face of the residence, edging the deck as a vertical element and, as a horizontal device, guiding movement to either end of its curved length. Resisting the temptation to step directly down from the living area to the lawn, this wall is a final layer through or around which one must pass to gain the site's promise.

ABOVE: *Looking north, the arced wall activates an energy between architecture and landscape. As with many SSA projects, the walls straddle an ambiguous line between being a horizontal datum against which one reads terrain, sky and water and being a vertical instrument that controls movement through the site, a barrier or threshold.*
OPPOSITE PAGE: *The oval lawn, embraced by stone walls, serves as a play and event lawn elevated above the cove. Manipulation of the lawn grade is subtle but critical to the perception of site and context.*

The second wall originates flush with the decking on the south corner of the house, then swings toward the pier. Its wide bluestone cap, a continuation of the detailing on the adjacent deck, invites one to stroll out along the arced length. The top-of-wall width tapers as the wall moves away from the house and as its height increases — a subtle trick that strengthens the effects of forced perspective. Syntheses of walkway, boundary, and artful object, the walls instigate a fluid gesture that grounds the house and embraces the convex contours emanating toward the shoreline. This residential landscape makes a careful distinction between the manmade and nature's work. In doing so, it ignites a vibrant tension not of opposites but of two entities skillfully counterbalanced in the service of graceful utility.

ABOVE: *The use of wood extends from within the residence out to the decking and renovated pier.*
RIGHT: *The wide walls guide movement to the sides of the deck but also invite one to experience them as a walkway or a seat.*
OPPOSITE PAGE: *Site plan.*

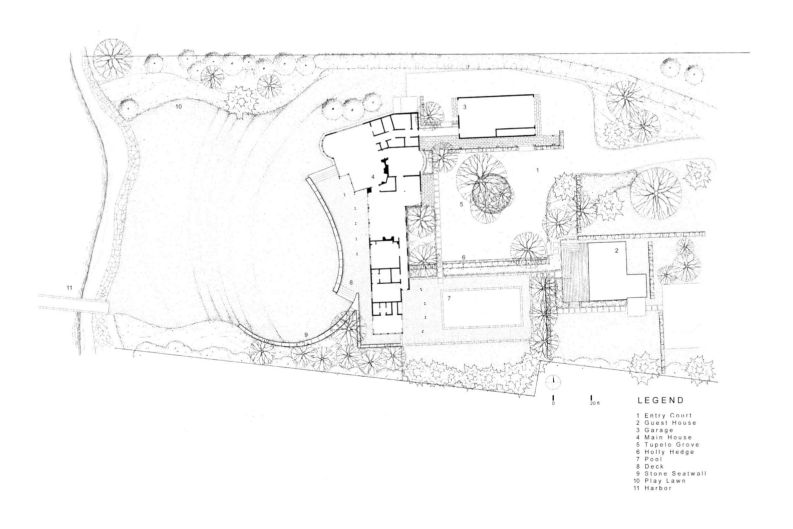

LEGEND

1 Entry Court
2 Guest House
3 Garage
4 Main House
5 Tupelo Grove
6 Holly Hedge
7 Pool
8 Deck
9 Stone Seatwall
10 Play Lawn
11 Harbor

0   20 ft

ABOVE: *The arc walls are constructed of split flat rough bluestone with a lilac bluestone cap. Integrated detailing defines the entire design, from the manner in which the wood deck meets stone to the bullnosed wall cap.*

OPPOSITE PAGE: *There is a purposeful shifting of planes from interior to exterior spaces. Grade changes tend to occur at gates, walls and transitions. Clear geometries strengthen the link between architecture and site and foster a visual energy that pulls one through the landscape.*

ABOVE RIGHT: *In the entry court native forest gives way to a legible destination defined by hedge lines, trees, pergola and paving.*

RIGHT: *Looking from the pool back toward the entry court, vertical planes or layered elements pull the eye with varying colors and textures.*

OPPOSITE PAGE: *Stones read equally as a cadenced edge and a walkway. Planted boundaries frame views and give privacy. A delicate custom wood and bronze gate leads from entry court to pool terrace.*

FOLLOWING PAGE: *The swimming pool borders are planted with blue and lilac perennials.*

PROJECT CREDITS

Stamper Garden, California
Contractor: Owner
Stacked wood wall construction: Anthony Rodrigues, Bruce Stamper
Black granite stone boundary sculpture: Edwin Hamilton (represented by New Leaf
 Gallery, 510-525-7621
Gardener: Anthony Rodrigues, Bruce Stamper
Materials: Paving at pool deck: French limestone; Paving at entry: decomposed granite;
 Rails: powder-coated metal stanchions; Pool: tempered glass panel
Significant plant material: Quercus virginiana; Miscanthus sinensis "Gracillimus";
 Bambusa oldhamii

Greenwich Garden, Connecticut
Contractor: Owner
Materials: Walls: stainless steel, white concrete; Paving: asphalt; Entrance paving:
 flamed black granite, polished black granite, and stainless steel
Significant plant material: Fagus sylvatica atropurpurea; Calmagrotis "Karl Foster";
 Busux sempervirens

Hatch Garden, California
Contractor: T. Delaney, Inc.
Materials: Party wall: white concrete, pure pigment stain; Stucco wall by spa: integral
 color; Wall surrounding garden: 2x12 redwood stained with pure pigment;
 Paving: decomposed granite
Surface ornament: mussel shells, abalone shells, conch shells
Significant plant material: Queen pams, Syagrus romanzoffianum

Pacific Garden, California
Contractor: T. Delaney, Inc./Jose Hildago
Concrete planters: Mary Collins
Materials: Deck: ipe planks; Rails: stainless steel; Stairs: ipe and integral color concrete;
Walls: integral color stucco; Bench: integral color concrete; Light cones at deck area:
 handmade fiberglass sheathing; Light shades at garden area: handmade
 Chinese lanterns with gut and epoxy
Significant plant material: Bambusa oldhamii; Brugmansia candida; white standard;
 Citrus; Bougainvillea; Ensete ventricosum; Neomarica caerulea; Phoenix
 Canarieusis in pots; Juncus "Quartz Creek" on descending steps;
 Sedum"Vera Jameson"; Carex testcea; Carex buhauii

Gupta Garden, California
Contractor: Jose Hildago
Lighting: brazier with charcoal, brazier with wood
Materials: Walls: Rastra foam with footings; Surface: La Habra acrylic stucco; Pavings:
 desert palm gravel
Significant plant material: Michelia doltsopa; Salvia leucantha; germaniums; Lavender
 prineta

Harlequin Garden, California
Contractor: T. Delaney, Inc./Jose Hildago
Materials: Paving: Buddy Rhoades Studio (415-641-8070); Planters: tempered steel;
 Walls: tempered steel, mirror; Glass: residual cullet
Significant plant materials: Sally Holmes roses; Phoenix Canariensis; Dasylirion

Goldfarb Garden, California
T. Delaney, Inc.; consultant Pam Anela Messanger
Contractor: Richard Colton (Berkeley, CA)
Materials: Wall: used brick veneers, mirror; Paving: brick; Rails: cast iron b Robinson
 Iron Works; Spiral stairs: original cast iron by Robinson Iron Works
Significant plant life: Ficus

Hotel Kohjimachi Kaikan, Tokyo
Client: Ministry of Home Affairs
Location: 2-4-3 Hirakawa-cho Chiyoda-ku Tokyo
Architect: Sato Sougou Keikaku
Contractor: Takenaka Corporation
Landscape contractor: Hibiya Amenis (cooperated with Shinichi Sano, Uetoh Zoen)
Stone works: Masatoshi Izumi

Imabari Kokusai Hotel, Ehime
Client: Imabari Shipbuilding Co., Ltd.
Location: 2-3-4 Asahi-machi Imabari city Ehime
Architect: Kanko Kikaku Sekkeisha, Naniwa Sekkei
Contractor: Shimizu Corporation
Landscape contractor: Shinichi Sano, Uetoh Zoen, and Masatoshi Izumi (stone work)

Hanoura Information/Culture Center, Tokushima
Client: Hanoura town
Location: Hanoura Nakagun, Tokushima
Architect: Ishimoto Architectural & Engineering Firm, Inc.
Contractor: Oobayashi Corporation
Landscape contractor: Oobayashi Corporation in cooperation with Matsuyama
Ryokuchi Kensetsu

Kagawa Prefecture Library, Takamatsu
Client: Kagawa Prefecture
Location: Hayashi-cho Takamatsu city
Architect: Ishimoto Architectural & Engineering Firm, Inc.
Contractor: Kajima Corporation
Landscape contractor: Kajima Corporation in cooperation with Masatoshi Izumi (stone
 work) and five landscape contractors

Canadian Museum of Civilization, Canada
Client: Canadian Museum of Civilization
Location: 100 Laurier Street Hull, Quebec, Canada
Architect: Douglas Cardinal
Local consultant: Don Vaughn Ltd.
Landscape contractor: Shinichi Sano, Uetoh Zoen, and a Canadian local contractor

University of British Columbia, Canada
Client: University of British Columbia
Location: Southwest Marine Drive, Vancouver, Canada
Local consultant: Don Vaughn Ltd.
Landscape contractor: Shinichi Sano, Uetoh Zoen, Double V Construction Ltd.
(Canada)

National Research Institute for Metals, Science and Technology Agency, Ibaragi
Client: Metals, Science and Technology Agency
Location: 1-2 Sengen Tsukuba city, Ibaragi
Architect: Nihon Sekkei Inc. and RIA
Contractor: Hazama Corporation
Landscape contractor: Hazama Corporation in cooperation with Masatoshi Izumi (stone work) and Hibiya Amenis

Niigata Prefectural Museum of Modern Art, Niigata
Client: Niigata Prefecture
Location: Nagaoka city, Niigata
Architect: Nihon Sekkei Inc.
Contractor: Taisei Corporation
Landscape contractor: Taisei Corporation in cooperation with 11 landscape contractors

Denenchofu Park Condominium, Tokyo
Client: Mitsui Real Estate Co.
Location: 2-26-27 Denenchoufu Oota, Tokyo
Architect: Tokyo Design Center/Genzaburoh Yamanaka
Contractor: Takenaka Corporation
Landscape contractor: Mitsui Greentech

Letham Grange Hotel and Golf Course, Scotland
Client: Letham Grange Hotel and Golf Course
Location: Colliston, Angus, Scotland
Landscape constractor: Shinichi Sano (Uetoh Zoen)

Manor Farm House, England
Client: Michael Balston
Location: Devizes, Wiltshire, England

Little Malvern Court, England
Client: Mrs. & Mr. T. M. Berington
Location: Little Malvern, Worcestershire, England
Contractor: M. Walsh & Son (Malvern) Ltd.

Jannaways, England
Client: The Honorable & Mrs. Christopher Sharples
Location: Berkshire, England
Contractor: Thames Water

Rofford Manor, England
Client: Mr. & Mrs. J. Mogford
Location: Little Milton, Oxfordshire, England
Landscape contractor: Client organization

Cucklington House, England
Client: Private
Location: Somerset, England
General contractor: Bayford Builders, Ltd.
Groundworks contractor: Newbridge Plant Services (1984) Ltd.
Landscape contractor: Johnstone Landscapes and client staff

Heather's Farm, England
Client: Mr. & Mrs. C. Gregson
Location: West Sussex, England
Groundworks contractor: Murwest Services AG
Landscape contractor: Landmark

Lower Lye, England
Client: Mr. & Mrs. A. Scott
Location: Somerset, England
Architects: Nicholas Johnston & Peter Cave Associates
General contractor: G. J. Smith Bros.
Groundworks contractor: Mike Lock Construction
Landscape contractor: Bob Carter

A London Garden, England
Client: Private
Location: London, England
Main contractor: Thomas Williams Ltd.
Landscape contractor: Leveson Landscapes

The Grange, England
Client: Mr. & Mrs. W. Caldwell
Location: West Sussex, England
Contractor: Client staff

Daily Telegraph Garden, England
Client: The Daily Telegraph
Location: Wisley, Surrey, England
Landscape contractor: Hillier Landscapes
Consulting engineers: Buro Happold
Engineering contractor: Landrell Fabric Engineering

Tezozomoc Park, Mexico
Client: Azcapotzalco Delegation, Tulio Hernández and Sergio Matínez, delegates
Location: Azcapotzalco, Mexico City, Mexico
Design and construction supervision: Mario Schjetnan Garduño, Jose Luis Pérez
Collaborators: Jorge Calvillo Lake and irrigation system: Mario Schjetnan Dantán
Area: 74.13 acres

Malinalco House, Mexico
Client: Mrs. Romero de Schjetnan
Location: Malinalco, Mexico
Design and construction supervision: Mario Schjetnan Garduño
Collaborators: Jorge Calvillo, Manuel Peniche, and Jose Luis Pérez
Area: 1,110 m2

Museum of Modern Art, Mexico
Client: Education and Culture Department of State of Mexico
Project direction: Mario Schjetnan Garduño, José Luis Pérez/Gonzalo Gomez Palacio
Advisor: Miriam Kaiser
Stone mural: Luis Nishizawa

Mexican Cultural Center, Mexico
Client: Education and Culture Department of State of Mexico
Location: Toluca, Mexico
Project direction: Mario Schjetnan Garduño, José Luis Pérez
Project for the Museum of Arts and Crafts: Mario Schjetnan Garduño, José Luis Pérez,
	Victor Monsivais
Project for the History and Anthropology Museum: Pedro Ramirez Vazquez and
	Amdres Giovanni García
Advisors: Mtra. Miriam Kaiser
Stone fountain: Luis Nishisawa and Mario Schjetnan

Culhuacán Historical Park, Mexico
Client: Culhuacán Community Center
Location: Iztapalapa, Mexico City, Mexico
Design and construction supervisor: Mario Schjetnan Garduño, José Luis Pérez
Archaeological direction: Elsa Hernández, archaeologist
History advisor: Juan Venegas, historian
Area: 2.471 acres

Malinalco Golf Club, Mexico
Client: Malinalco Golf Club, S.A. de C.V.
Design and construction supervisor: Mario Schjetnan Garduño, José Luis Pérez
Collaborators: Marco Arturo González
Area: 425.012 acres

Fountains, Mexico
Client: Desarrollos Immobiliarios Delta (DID), Ing. Federico Garza Santos
Location: Monterrey, Nuevo León
Project direction: Arqs. Mario Schjetnan, José Luis Pérez/Grupo de Diseño Urbano S.C.
Architectural design: DID/Camargo Architects
Sculpture fountain: Mahia Biblos, Mario Schjetnan
Project management: PLATE Administración de Proyectos
Collaborators: Arq. Miguel Camacho (GDU), Arq. Alejandro Lira (GDU)
		Arq. José Luis Gómez
Area: 7,300 m2

Archaeological Museum of the Northern Cultures of Mexico, Mexico
Client: Instituto Nacional de Antropologia e Historia
Location: Paquimé Casa Grandes, Bhihuahua, Mexico
Design and construction supervisor: Mario Schjetnan Garduño, José Luis Pérez
Archaeology and history direction: Beatriz Braniff, archaeologist
Collaborators: Ricardo Sánchez, Socorro Alatorre, Arturo Sotomayor, José Luis
Gómez, Pablo Romero, Alfredo Arnada, Francisco Ibañez, Salvador Escalante
Museography: Jorge Agostoni

Spanish Tropical Garden, Florida
Landscape contractor: Stan Matthews, Plant Creations Soils: sandy loam topsoil over
	oolitic limestone
General contractor for pool house and re-creation pavilion: Walter Daggett
Lighting: Kim and B-K fixtures, Perry Kuhn, lighting consultant
Area: 210 by 120 foot lot

Sims Garden, Florida
General contractors: Action Builders
Landscape contractor: Stan Matthews, Plant Creations Soils: organic topsoil over
	oolitic limestone
Lighting: HADCO, Lumiere, and Kim fixtures

Cascade Pool, Massachusetts
Project manager: Richard Johnson, SSA
Architect: Hart Associates
General contractor: Thoughtforms Corp., Aquaknot Pools, Inc.
Landscape contractors: R. P. Marzilli & Company, Inc., Hayden Hillgrove
Structural engineer: LeMessurier Consultants, Inc.
Artist: Rosalind Waters

Hawk Rise, Massachusetts
Project manager: Richard Johnson, SSA
Architect: S. A. Perry Architects, Inc.
General contractor: Thirty Acre Wood, LLC
Landscape contractor: Francisco Tavares, Inc.
Pool contractor: Luziette Pool and Spa, Inc.
Tree Mover: Instant Shade, Inc.
Metalsmith: Sebastien Richer, Richer Metal

Cove House, Massachusetts
Project manager: Kim Mercurio, SSA
Architect: Thompson & Rose Architect, Inc.
General contractor: Gentile Remodeling
Landscape contractor: R. P. Marzilli and Company, Inc.
Pool contractor: Custom Quality Pools, Inc.
Metalsmith: Cape Cod Fabrications, Inc.

CREDITS

Michael Balston & James Balston, 8 (left); 166-175; 176-183; 184-191; 192-203; 204-213; 214-223; 234-237; 238-249

Michael Calderwood, Boris de Swan, Gabriel Figueroa & Tom Lamb /Mario Schjetnan, 254-259

Topher Delaney, Inc., Seam Studio, 20-29; 32 (top); 44-51; 64

Gabriel Figueroa/Mario Schjetnan, 260-269; 286-291

Gabriel Figueroa, Tom Lamb, & Arturo Zavala/Mario Schjetnan, 280-285

Gabriel Figueroa & Alfonso Muñoz/Mario Schjetnan, 292-297

Gabriel Figueroa, Jorge Sandoval/Mario Schjetnan, 276-279

Loretta Gargan/Topher Delaney, Inc., Seam Studio, 32 (bottom)

Jerry Harpur, Michael Balston, & James Balston, 250-253

Haruo Hirota/Shunmyo Masuno, 102-109; 110-117; 126-135; 136-143; 144-151

Shunmyo Masuno, 118-125; 160-165

Charles Mayer/Stephen Stimson Associates, 318-327; 328-337; 338-346

Ira Nowinski/Topher Delaney, Inc., Seam Studio, 10-19; 33; 35; 43; 58; 66-82

Lanny Provo/Raymond Jungles, 8 (right); 298-309; 310-317

Ian Reeves/Topher Delaney, Inc., Seam Studio, 30-31; 52-53; 60; 62; 65

Gráfico: Brian L. Rothman/Mario Schjetnan, 276-279

Jorge Sandoval & Gonzalo Gómez Palacios/Mario Schjetnan, 270-275

Minao Tabata/Shunmyo Masuno, 84-91; 92-101

Tokyo Design Center/Shunmyo Masuno, 152-159

Kelli Yon/Topher Delaney, Inc., Seam Studio, 34; 36-41; 54-57; 61; 63

FIRM DIRECTORY

Michael Balston
Balston & Company
Long Barn, Patney,
Devizes, Wiltshire
SN10 3RB
England
Phone: 1380848181
Fax: 1380484189
E-mail: admin@balston.co.uk

Topher Delaney
T. Delaney, Inc./Seam Studio
600 Illinois Street
San Francisco, CA 94107
Phone: (415) 621-9899
Fax: (415) 896-2995
E-mail: topher@tdelaney.com

Raymond Jungles
Raymond Jungles DIC
517 Duval Street, #206
Key West, Florida 33040
Phone: (305) 294-6700
Fax: (305) 294-6494
E-mail: Raymond@raymondjungles.com

Shunmyo Masuno
Japan Landscape Consultants, Ltd.
Kenkohji 1-2-1 Baba Tsurumi-ku
Yokohama city
Phone: 45-571-5204
Fax: 45-571-5201
E-mail: kenkohji@courante.plala.on.jp

Mario Schjetnan
Grupo de Digero Urbano
F. Moules de Oca. #4
Col. Condesa, Mexico City, D.F.
06140
Phone: 52 55 55 53 12 48
Fax: 52 55 55 52 86 10 13
E-mail: cotteo@gdu.com.mx

Steven Stimpson
Steven Stimpson Associates
15 Depot Avenue
Falmouth, MA 02540
Phone: (508) 548-8119
Fax: (508) 548-7718